# Coming Home Again

*Danette Fogarty*

What does a 32 year old successful mystery/suspense writer do when she's at the top of her game? She leaves Los Angeles and buys a house in her hometown, of course. Aubrey Slojankonkowski, aka A.J. Sloan, has been writing best sellers for years, but now, when everyone wants a piece of her or at least her fame, she wants solitude. Moving home to Burlington, Wisconsin is the perfect solution, or is it? She finds the perfect house, but it hides a secret, a secret that Aubrey discovers, she must solve. If only her contractor, Cole Rafferty wasn't so hunky, maybe she could concentrate on getting out another best seller and solving the real-life mystery in front of her.

Cole Rafferty had known Aubrey's parents for years, but hadn't had the opportunity to meet their famous-writer daughter. She was so much more than just a pretty face, although that particular part of her captivated him too. She was out to prove herself, just as he was, that they were a force to be reckoned with, in their chosen careers.

Could these two people, so alike and so different, find the one thing they both craved.......love?

# Chapter 1

Christmas Eve, 1956

Maddie cautiously walked to the back of the warehouse, the only sound in the dark was of her shoes, crunching on the newly fallen snow. She had gotten William's note and, ever so carefully, followed his instructions. She didn't let anyone know she was meeting him at his factory on the edge of downtown Burlington.

As the note stated, she found the back door was unlocked. She pushed it open, her heart racing as the old hinges squeaked, and sending echoes through the empty space. Although she was told no one would be here, she still worried.

There was no source of light inside, adding to Maddie's uneasiness. After a few minutes her eyes began to adjust to the darkness. She managed to find a lamp and flipped it on. Finding herself in the back offices of the factory, she gingerly made her way through the hallway, and toward a flight of stairs that led to where William's office was located.

Her footsteps were slow and began to echo louder as the snow on the bottom of her shoes started to melt. She wrapped her arms around herself to fight off the bitter cold that seeped into her bones.

The big building seemed ominous in the darkness.

She'd been here before, she recalled with fondness, with William's daughter, Eileen. They'd walked through the big factory so Eileen could visit her father during a school holiday. It had been so much fun, to see Eileen holding her father's hand, and walking among the machines, listening intently to her father's explanation of which machines did what. Maddie smiled at the memory, realizing that was the first time she felt the pang of feelings for Mr. William McIntyre. He'd always been kind to her, allowing her to have some fun with little Eileen.

As Maddie made her way upstairs, she felt a cold shudder come across her body and immediately thought of William's wife, Mrs. Marion McIntyre.

If ever there was a soulless creature, Maddie was sure it was Marion McIntyre. Even a nanny, with only a basic understanding of the world, could see that the woman held not a single scrap of love for either her husband or child. Marion McIntyre was a woman who knew only one love; money.

There were times when Maddie actually pitied Mrs. McIntyre, but then Marion would use words in such a way, to a staff member or family member that would make Maddie angry. Coming from a loving family, though with little means, Maddie was brought up to believe that a person, no matter what their circumstances, was born decent. Marion McIntyre held no such belief and was the only person Maddie had ever wished ill will toward.

Reaching the top of the stairs, Maddie was surprised not to see any lights on. William's note specifically said he would be waiting for her in his office. Perhaps he just wanted to make sure no one saw the light. After all, his office did face the street allowing any passersby to see. With it being Christmas Eve, surely someone would investigate why a light was on in a closed building.

Knocking the third door to the right, which she'd recalled as being William's, Maddie listened intently for any sound.

Slowly, she pushed open the door. The office was quiet, dark, still, and held no signs that anyone was there.

Confused, Maddie quickly looked down the hallway, hoping for some sign of the man she loved.

Suddenly, there was a noise, and Maddie stood frozen with fear. The sound resonated from somewhere downstairs so she darted into William's office and closed the door quietly behind her.

If it was William, she'd wait patiently, but she wasn't sure if there might be a security guard who patrolled the building or, heaven forbid, a policeman noticing unusual footprints in the snow leading up to the back door.

Fear and excitement ran through her body as Maddie waited, her ears straining for any noise that could mean either William was coming to her, or her worst nightmare, someone else discovering her there.

When she'd found the note from William in her room, she'd been so overwhelmed with excitement. Two months earlier, she and William confessed their feelings for one another, and it was liberating.

Marion happened to be out of town for one of her social functions, leaving William and Eileen in the care of the staff. One evening, after having some wine, William sat in the living room, and spoke to Maddie not as an employee, but as a friend.

He asked her opinion on a variety of topics and she was delighted that they were of a similar opinion on many topics. It was like she found her perfect match.

Perhaps it was the wine, or maybe the loneliness they both felt, but he'd kissed her.

At first, he was apologetic and promised that he would never cross the line again, but Maddie had reassured him that no line had been crossed and that she was not only pleased with the kiss, but asked him to kiss her again.

Their love affair consisted of little more than a series of late night rendezvous and stolen moments when little Eileen was at school or at a function with her mother.

Maddie knew it wasn't respectable, what she was doing, but her heart lightened every time she saw William. There was a kindness in his eyes that told her that he would always keep her safe.

Only the week before, William informed her that he'd finally retained an attorney out of Chicago, to help him get a divorce from Marion. He'd confided in Maddie that they married to join their families' businesses and there had never been love between them. Once Eileen was conceived, Marion then informed him that there would no longer be intimate relations between them, and it broke his heart. To William, even if he and his wife didn't share a love, at least they could love their children. With Marion unwilling to do that with him, he knew he could never love her.

Placing her hand over her belly protectively, Maddie smiled at his reaction when she told him she carried his child inside her. If Marion wouldn't bear his children, then Maddie would, and her happiness would be absolutely complete.

Knowing that he was going to divorce Marion made Maddie's heart lighten and her fear lessen. Little Eileen would come and live with them eventually, and she would have little brothers and sisters to dote on.

Maddie loved Eileen as if she were her own child now, so it would be perfect when all of them could be together.

Hearing another noise, Maddie quietly made her way to the door.  She leaned her ear against the cold wood, and listened.

She could discern footsteps coming down the hall and her heart sped up at the prospect that William was coming to be with her.

He'd probably just been delayed because he waited for Marion to go to bed before leaving the house.

The footsteps stopped outside the office door, and Maddie held her breath. With a rush of excitement, combined with fear, she waited, trembling.

Then, she heard a key in the lock, followed by a distinctive click.  Her heart literally stopped, all the excitement she felt seeping out of her.  She tried to open the door, but found it was locked from the outside.  She could hear the footsteps receding and going down the stairs.

On the verge of panic, Maddie tried to knock softly on the door, wondering why someone would only lock this particular door.  When she received no answer, she knocked a little louder......still nothing.

Going over to the window, Maddie looked down.  The street was dark and deserted.  Then, she noticed a single pair of headlights as they pulled out onto the street. With a sense of dread, she realized they were leaving the factory.

Now Maddie was really confused. She waved her hands frantically in the window, knowing full well that someone in a car wouldn't see her up on the second story. The car looked like William's but that made no sense since he was the one who asked her to meet him here.

She turned around and plopped down into the desk chair behind the massive desk. Her eyes started welling up and she started breathing heavily. None of this made sense! Maddie wanted to cry because she just couldn't understand.

Not caring if someone saw her, she reached over to turn on the desk lamp. For whatever reason, it wouldn't turn on. There was enough moonlight pouring into the room for her to make out the furniture and Maddie felt as if the shadows they created were going to swallow her up.

She didn't know how long she stayed like that, sitting in the dark, and must have dozed off because she woke up a while later, her mind still rushing.

Something was wrong, that much was obvious. Her insides were all knotted and her mind was on high alert and Maddie just didn't know why she felt this way.

Maybe William had showed up? She got up and walked over to the door to listen once again. But, as soon as her fingers made contact with the heavy wood door, they felt heat coming off of it. That was odd because the room was cool.

When she stepped back, Maddie could now see little wisps of smoke seeping below the bottom of the door. Her mind and body kicked into a state of desperation; she started pounding on the door. "Help!" She cried out.

A few minutes later, the door was too hot for her to touch, and Maddie moved further back into the office. She noticed another door to what she assumed was, an adjacent office, but it too was locked. The smoke was now pouring into the space, making it difficult for her to see. Her breathing was now becoming more challenging as well.

Looking around, Maddie found a blanket or jacket hanging over the back of a chair. She grabbed it and stuffed it into the bottom of the door, trying to seal it so the smoke would stop coming into the office.

After that was done, she ran over to the window, and tried to open it up. It wouldn't budge. Again, her heart skipped a beat as she remembered it was open just a few weeks beforehand when William was waving to Eileen as she left to go on a trip with Maddie and her mother.

Running her fingers across the top of the window, Maddie felt something sharp slice into her fingertips. With the adrenalin running through her, she didn't feel the blood coming out of the cuts. She was just desperate in her attempts to get the window open.

Maddie started to bang her palms on the glass, seeing them smudge with the blood from her fingertips. She didn't care, she just frantically wanted to get out! "Help!" She screamed, her voice sounding hoarse from the smoke in the room.

She could hear crackling now, and knew the fire was just outside the door. Not knowing where it originated, she had no idea how long it would be until it invaded the office, she only knew that, if she didn't get out, she would die.

"William!" She screamed, tears now pouring down her cheeks. "Help me!"

There was no answer.

Trying to think, her mind jumbled, Maddie suddenly remembered there was a phone in the room. She would call for help, and William would come and save her.

Tripping as she made her way around the desk, she groped the surface, and sighed in relief when her hand found the telephone. Picking up the receiver, Maddie started to turn the rotary when she heard no dial tone. The line wasn't working so there would be no call for help.

The temperature in the room was rising, she could feel it the heat radiating from the door. Escape, it seemed, was impossible now.

Lying in a ball, near the window, Maddie started praying.

She prayed that this was a bad dream and she would wake up to see William and Eileen waiting for her. They would move away from here, and find a small house in the country and have babies and be happy.

Protectively covering her belly, Maddie prayed that God keep her unborn child safe.

She could now hear the flames licking at the walls, and knew, with certainty, that she would not live to see tomorrow.

Crying, she shed tears for her parents, her brothers, little Eileen, and especially for William.

The smoke wound its way past her makeshift stop gap and was now pouring into the room, making breathing more difficult by the second. Maddie kept herself low to the ground, desperately trying to stay alive long enough for help to come. She knew William wouldn't do this to her. She had to believe that, or everything she loved would have been a lie.

As Maddie lay on the floor of the office, she heard an explosion. The whole building vibrated with it, and she was sure the floor would give way.

There was sweat pouring out of her pores, the heat was so intense! She stayed where she was, just below the window. Hoping. Praying.

Finally, the flames appeared, from beneath the door that led to the adjacent office. She knew these would be her final minutes, and prayed that the fire department would find her in time.

Were those sirens? Maddie strained to hear them in the distance, hope once again filling up her chest. Help was on the way....thank God.

She thought, for a moment, that she would be back in William's arms very soon.

Peering out the window, but still staying as low as she could, and still breathe, she saw the first fire engine pull up to the end of the building. She could see the flames dancing in and out of the windows on the ground floor. Oh, the sight of it frightened her.

She pounded on the window, hoping beyond hope that someone would see her, hear her, or realize someone was in the building.

"Help," She croaked out. Her voice was barely audible now.

Slumping back down against the wall, her hand down the glass window. Maddie said her very last prayer.

She prayed William and Eileen would have a happy life, even if it wouldn't include her. They deserved happiness at the very least.

Her breathing was extremely shallow now, with the taste of ash filling her mouth. The floor was steaming, burning her skin where it made contact.

Maddie felt a certain peace in the thought of death. This was not a way that anyone should die! She hoped to see Heaven soon and prayed for an end to this pain and suffering.

The floor started to buckle, and with her last breath, Maddie closed her eyes. She waited. The floor gave way and plunged her into the inferno below.

# Chapter 2

April, 2015

Welcome to

Burlington, Wisconsin

Chocolate City, USA

Aubrey smiled as she drove southbound on Hwy 36 into her hometown. The sign always made her smile, that and the smell of chocolate. Although the smell wasn't present today, she knew it would be there at some point.

The drive from California was exhausting, but she'd been determined to do it. Her little, light blue convertible wasn't going to do well during the harsh Wisconsin winters, but she wanted to hang on to it for a little longer. Plus, driving it through the desert of Southern California, through Arizona, New Mexico, Texas, Oklahoma, Missouri, Illinois, and finally into Wisconsin had been wonderful.

Driving into Burlington, Aubrey noticed that things were different now, and she experienced her first ping of apprehension. What used to be farmland only a decade earlier, was now developed into strip malls, a huge car dealership, and chain stores. Not that having those conveniences was bad, it was just different.

Slowing down for traffic, she passed restaurants and places she'd hung out in during high school. The late spring weather was perfect for driving slow, with the convertible top down so she could see the places that made up a lot of memories. She passed the old Lynch car dealership, remembering the first car her parents bought her. Passing Echo Lake, with baseball diamonds just across the street, Aubrey smiled and remembered cheering her dad on during the years he played softball.

On her left, the sign for Adrian's Frozen Custard gleamed in the late-morning light. She made a mental note to go there as soon as possible to get a twist cone. They made the best frozen custard in the country as far as she was concerned.

There was a new Veteran's Center on the right side of the street, and it looked great. Her dad always told her they needed a bigger venue with the growth Burlington had seen in recent years.

As she pulled up to the light that started the "downtown" area, Aubrey studied the buildings. Some dated back to the 1800's, when Burlington was first settled by the Mormons on their way west. These were the best, in her book. The light turned green so she continued on. The old movie house was now a 4-Plex, wow!

Turning left onto Kane Street, where the downtown businesses receded into residential neighborhoods. There were large trees that lined the street and some very large homes in this part of town. Old Victorians meshed with newer remodels and Aubrey remembered walking down this street with friends after grade school.

Her father was a doctor here so he knew a lot of people. Being a General Practitioner, he would see multiple generations in families and, in turn, Aubrey and her mother, met and befriended a lot of them.

Living in California for the last ten plus years, it was hard to remember the quiet of small city life. Of course, she wagered that if she asked some of the longer term residents here, they would complain about the growth in Burlington as much as she complained about the congestion of Orange County and Los Angeles.

At last, she came to the street she was looking for, Duane Street, with its big houses, and large city lots. Being only a block away from the hospital, there were a few doctors who resided in the neighborhood, with their neatly tended lawns and grand looking homes.

Turning right onto the street, Aubrey's heart started beating faster.

Her friends in California thought she was nuts, buying a house without physically seeing it first.

Personally, Aubrey thought it was the not-knowing part that made it fun. She was a mystery suspense writer after all, she was a master of "revealing" things in due course. Not to mention, her parents had seen it first hand and assured her it was a good purchase.

She parked across the street from the house and got out of her car slowly, allowing the full force of the view to draw her in.

It was a large house, a Dutch Colonial. As soon as she'd seen it on the real estate website, Aubrey knew it was the one for her.

Even though she could certainly afford something much grander, she chose this house. Her friends and colleagues in California kept asking, "Why don't you buy an estate in the mountains?" Sighing as she stepped toward her new home, Aubrey knew it was because this was for her and her alone. The rat race of California was great while she was a struggling writer, but now, she needed something more.

"Well, if it isn't the big-time writer!" Her father shouted as he stepped out of the front door of the house.

Smiling, Aubrey practically ran over to him, "Dad," she hugged him, squeezing him tight. When her dad held her like this, she felt like a little girl.

Setting his daughter a step back from him, Greg searched her face wanting to see for himself that she was alright. Maybe it was because he was a doctor, but he worried. "You look tired," He said to her.

Aubrey rolled her eyes, "You'd be tired too if you spent two and a half days driving halfway across the country, Dad."

Laughing, Greg nodded, and answered, "I guess so."

He stepped aside and motioned for his daughter to go inside the house.

As soon as Aubrey entered the house, she smelled the very distinctive smell of animal urine, and crinkled her nose.

The entryway had gorgeous wood floors. It was narrow, with a small coat closet across from the front door, and the stairs that led to the 2nd floor. Her father led her to the right, and into the formal dining room. It had white, yes white, carpet and was stained with, what she assumed, was the cause of the unpleasant smell.

As she entered the dining room, she was met by her realtor, a nice lady, named Peggy, who helped her find the house.

"Ms. Slojankonkowski, how are you?" Peggy asked her, a bright smile pasted on her face.

Smiling in return, Aubrey answered, "I'll be great once I can get the closing done and get to the renovations."

Peggy nodded, "Well, let's go then," and she turned to lead Aubrey and her father into the kitchen.

It was a small, room, but held a decent amount of cupboard space. The real draw was the breakfast nook beyond it. Aubrey walked past where Peggy was explaining the condition of the appliances and stood next to the bank of windows that overlooked the backyard. There was a built-in window seat below them, which made Aubrey smile.

Greg walked over and stood beside his daughter. He knew her mind was miles away, thinking of whatever popped into it at the moment. It was one of the things that took him a long time to understand about his little girl; she just did things her own way. "Are you okay?" He asked her after a minute.

Aubrey was jolted out of her thoughts, and looked over at her dad, "I was just thinking how nice this will be when I'm writing."

Nodding, Greg smiled, and added, "We should probably finish the walk-through so you can sign the papers and get to your view."

Even though she didn't want to move, Aubrey nodded in agreement and walked back to where the, eager looking, Peggy was standing.

They went through the kitchen, discussing appliances, briefly touched on the breakfast nook, which had red carpet and an ugly green paint on the built in cupboards.

Around the corner was the back door on the right, and two doors on the left.

Peggy opened the door, and they walked out onto a large back deck. The lot, although narrow, was deep, and

Aubrey knew she'd love to put in a fire pit for night time. The trees in the back of the yard were mature evergreens and provided a natural fence, along with privacy.

Peggy pointed over to their right, and Aubrey cringed. The garage had definitely seen better days. It leaned precariously to the left and Aubrey knew it would need to be torn down completely and rebuilt.

Going back inside, Aubrey and her father followed Peggy into the narrow hallway. When Peggy opened up the first of the two doors, Aubrey started laughing.

"Now, that's what I call a water closet," She said, and stepped back so her dad could peek inside.

Indeed, there was actually a toilet, and just a toilet, in the closet. "Oh my," Greg said, and chuckled.

Peggy, clearly not as amused as they were, cleared her throat, closed the door, and turned to open the one next to it.

After flipping on the switch, Peggy proceeded to lead the way downstairs to the basement.

One of the first things that Aubrey noticed, was that there was a lot of natural light down here. As she reached the basement floor, she realized the previous owner had renovated it into another family room. There were a ton of built-in cabinets along the walls, and that intrigued her. It was obvious that someone liked organization. Other than the wall color and the carpet color, Aubrey thought the room was cozy.

Peggy led them into the utility room, where the furnace, hot water heater, and washer and dryer were located. It hadn't been renovated, but didn't need to be either. Aubrey did notice that the furnace looked newer, as did the hot water heater.

They walked back through the "family room" and into what was a bedroom with an en suite bathroom.

"This is great!" Aubrey said, "When my agent comes, I can stick her down here."

Greg laughed, knowing that Aubrey was joking, but that there were probably days when she wanted to tuck her agent into a basement dungeon.

As they made their way back toward the stairs up to the first floor, Aubrey noticed a door on the far side of the family room. "What's that?" She asked Peggy.

Peggy frowned, "It's just a fruit cellar," she replied and continued toward the stairs.

"I'm going to look at it," Aubrey stated in an authoritarian voice.

Greg tried to keep from smiling. Another trait his daughter possessed was the ability to reduce others into a state of obedience with merely a look.

Aubrey walked over, unhooked the latch on the, smaller than average, door and opened it. The creek of the wood was enough to send a chill up her spine.

Peggy said, "There's a pull cord for a light to your right, there."

Since it was daytime, and at the far end of the room Aubrey noticed a narrow window, there was just enough light to find the light switch rope. She yanked and a single bulb came on in the middle of the room.

Creepy did not even begin to explain this room. As Peggy said, it was a fruit cellar. There was a dirt floor and shelves lining either side. But what made it creepy was there, in the middle of the room, sat a rocking chair. The room was completely devoid of anything except this rocking chair.

For a moment, Aubrey was drawn into the room. It was like stepping into a dream, the edges of her sight were fuzzy and she could clearly see, in the center of her gaze, a woman rocking in the chair, a child in her arms.

As quickly as the image appeared, it disappeared, and Aubrey stumbled back a step, and back out into the family room part of the basement.

"Are you okay?" Greg asked his daughter, concern creasing his brow.

Aubrey shook her head, and smiled, "I'm fine," she answered flatly, clearly an effort to play off the incident. She wasn't sure what just happened. Maybe it was just from traveling, she didn't know.

The trio went back upstairs and went through the rest of the house. There was a long living room that ran the depth of the house itself, with a screened-in porch that was accessible through French doors.

On the second floor, there were four bedrooms and one bathroom. Each room was small, except the master bedroom, which Aubrey could tell had been two separate rooms at one time.

"Oh my," She sighed as they entered the large space.

Peggy smiled, "It's huge isn't it?" She asked Aubrey, who nodded.

The only drawback, for Aubrey, was the two very small closets that were at both ends of the room. But it did have a French door that went out to a patio on top of the screened porch below.

Aubrey stepped out onto the patio and grimaced. "Yuck," She said to her father, after he'd joined her. "It's just tar."

Greg smiled and patted his daughter's shoulder, replying, "We'll fix it."

Peggy cleared her throat and announced, "Okay, that's it," before turning to go downstairs.

Greg and Aubrey laughed at her demeanor, but they both knew this sale was going to happen, this tour was just a formality.

After joining Peggy back in the kitchen, Aubrey signed all the necessary paperwork, and handed over the cashier's check for the negotiated price. Seeing her father's raised eyebrows, she shrugged, and said, "Sold a lot of books."

He smiled in return, then led Peggy to the door so she could be on her way.

Aubrey sat in the kitchen of the house she'd just bought, and wondered what happened downstairs in that room.

# Chapter 3

After the realtor left, Aubrey pulled her little blue car into the driveway and she and her dad took everything she'd managed to cram inside of it into the house.

They chatted about this and that, keeping it light. She knew there were questions her parents were going to ask her, she was just too tired right now to answer them. "Where's Mom?" She asked as they brought in the last of her suitcases.

Greg put the bags down in the living room area, and answered, "Oh, she'll be here any time. She had a meeting."

The word "meeting" held about 30 different meanings for Christine Slojankonkowski. Aubrey's mother was a spitfire of energy and put more effort into one day than most people did into three. She'd retired from nursing about five years earlier, only to be asked to sit on boards. First, it was the hospital fundraiser board, then other organizations came to the energetic and organized doctor's wife and asked her to assist with their fund raisers, etc.

Aubrey knew she, herself, routinely doled out money to dozens of foundations her mother had some hand in, but she didn't mind. Christine was always taking care of others, she just didn't do it in scrubs anymore.

"Speak of the angel," Greg said, and nodded toward the front door.

Aubrey smiled because he always called her mom, "Angel." As she looked out the window, following his gaze, her breath caught in her throat.

Her mother was coming down the front walk of the house, in a couture dress suit, with high heels and perfect hair. Aubrey thought she looked more like her sister, than her mother.

Seeing his daughter's reaction to her mother made Greg smile. He always thought his wife was the most beautiful woman on the planet, and now, everyone else was able to see it too.

Walking to the front door, Aubrey opened it up and just gawked at her mother, "Uh, can somebody say super model?" She asked to no one in particular.

Christine laughed, and took her daughter into her arms. There was nothing like holding your baby, and Christine had always adored holding her little girl. Even if her "little girl" was now over thirty years old, and a well-known, published author. "My girl," She whispered into her daughter's hair.

"Mommy," Aubrey whispered back.

As the women separated, and stepped inside the house, Greg stepped forward to give his wife a kiss.

Aubrey stepped out of the room, going into the kitchen, to give her parents a little privacy. From what she knew from her phone conversations with them, her parents didn't get a whole lot of private time. If she could give them a little of that, then she'd feel better about relying on them to help her buy the house.

"Now," Christine said as she walked into the kitchen, a minute later. "What do you think?" She asked her daughter.

Blowing out a breath, Aubrey replied, "I think I've made a good purchase, but there's a lot of work to be done."

Nodding at their little girl, Christine chimed in, "Yes!"

The three of them laughed, and went into the breakfast nook to sit on the window bench.

"I've got someone in mind for doing your contracting," Greg told Aubrey.

Aubrey was relieved. The thought of trying to find a reliable and reasonably priced contractor, when she hadn't lived here for years, seemed daunting. "That's great," She said to her dad, then asked him, "When can I meet him?"

Christine smiled at her daughter, and said, "Dad made you an appointment tomorrow morning, so you could get a good night's sleep at our house, and not feel rushed."

Looking at her parents' happy faces, Aubrey felt a little guilty. She smiled sheepishly, and told them, "Well, I think I'm just going to stay here."

Laughing, Christine thought the joke was funny. Then she saw the look on her daughter's face, and knew Aubrey was not kidding. She'd run into that look far too many times during Aubrey's childhood to not recognize determination. "Oh," Was all she said in return.

"Mom," Aubrey rushed, taking her mom's hand into her own, "It's not that I don't want to stay with you two, it's that this is MY place now, and I'd rather just dive in."

Greg understood, but he was pretty sure his wife didn't. She viewed their daughter's homecoming a little differently than he did, and he feared she would have her feelings bruised until she realized that Aubrey was truly grown up. "No problem, I'll bring over donuts and meet you here in the morning."

Not wanting to see the look of hurt on her mother's face, Aubrey asked her, "Then can you and I have lunch tomorrow?"

The question did perk up Christine's spirits. "Of course," She answered, and then calculated phone calls she'd have to make. "Do you want to have dinner with us tonight?" She asked hopefully.

"Actually," Aubrey responded, "I think I'm just going to grab a burger and then run over to the store to pick up some necessities before hitting the hay." She squeezed her mom's hand again.

Sighing, Christine nodded at her little girl, then stood up. "Okay, then," She looked at her husband, "Greg, it's just you and me, baby."

Wiggling his eyebrows at his wife, he then turned to wink at Aubrey, before responding, "Just the way I like it."

Aubrey walked her parents to the front door, and watched as her father escorted her mother to her car, tucked her inside, and waited for her to leave before getting into his own car. He waved as he pulled away, Aubrey raising her hand in return. She wondered if she would ever find a man that was as kind to her as her father was to her mother, then walked back into the house.

An hour later, a list in her hands, Aubrey left the house in search for furniture and some basic things she could use during the renovations.

Driving back through downtown, Aubrey took a right turn through the "loop," which was a right turn that looped around to Pine Street. She noticed that there was an Italian place called, Zumpano's on the corner, and made a note to stop in soon for a bite.

After getting back onto Pine Street, Aubrey drove down the block and finally found her first destination;

Fred's. She'd really wanted to stop for some frozen custard at Adrian's but her "grown up" side said, food first. She parked and went inside, feeling guilty the whole way. She should be eating better but it wasn't every day that you bought a house in a city you haven't lived in for over a decade, so she decided to cut herself some slack. Ordering a burger, she did refrain from getting a soda.

Sitting down, she almost melted into a puddle at the smell of the freshly cooked food. Realizing she'd forgotten to eat lunch, it was no wonder she was starving.

The burger was better than she remembered, and Aubrey figured her California friends would forgive her lapse in judgement just this once.

Her stomach full, Aubrey left the restaurant and turned back onto the main stretch leaving town.

A few minutes outside of town, she saw the huge Lynch dealership and knew she'd need to stop in soon to get her car maintenance and maybe look for something more practical, but that would have to wait.

Not ten minutes later, she was at Roesing's Furniture. Aubrey couldn't remember when it was built, it had been there so long. She figured this would be a one-stop shop to begin her new life in the house with.

She pulled into the parking lot, and was relieved that they were still open for several hours yet.

When she walked in, Aubrey smiled, yes, this would do very nicely. She made her way toward the dining room sets and started looking around.

About ten minutes later, a woman came up to her, and asked if she needed help. As soon as Aubrey looked up to acknowledge her, they both gasped in surprise. Aubrey asking, "Jess, is that you?"

"Aubrey?" Jess asked in reply, then laughed.

The two women hugged.

When Aubrey stepped back she shook her head in disbelief, then asked, "How are you?"

Jess laughed, and answered, "I'm good, and you?" She guided Aubrey over to a living room sectional and motioned for her to sit.

Not believing that she ran into one of her oldest high school friends, Aubrey started asking questions. "What have you been up to? Are you married? Do you have kids?"

Putting her hand over her old friend's hand, Jess smiled, and answered. "Lots, yes, yes."

Leave it to Jess to leave her hanging, Aubrey thought to herself. "Tell me everything!"

And Jess did, she told Aubrey about how she decided to go to college at the local community college in town, then met her, now husband, Joe. She delighted Aubrey with stories of their kids, Bethany, Ricky, and Tripp and even showed her old friend pics from her phone.

When Jess was done, Aubrey was flooded with a mix of emotions. She was, of course, happy, that she ran into her high school friend, but she was also a little sad.

"Your turn!" Jess said excitedly. "We know you're a big time writer, so spill, which celebrities do you know?" She asked Aubrey.

It was a bit of a stretch but, luckily, Aubrey had been fortunate to meet a few celebrities. She told Jess about finishing school at UCLA, then doing internships at publishing houses and shoving her manuscripts at anyone who would read them. Then, when her first published book hit the market, she'd decided to stay in California.

Jess listened intently, and asked a few questions here and there. "So, I have all your books," She said, and flushed. "I'm hooked!"

Blushing herself, Aubrey replied, "Thank you." She always felt giddy when a reader complimented her work. "I'll sign all of them if you'd like," She told Jess.

Holding her hand to her chest, Jess's mouth dropped open. "That would be great!" She exclaimed.

Standing up, Aubrey didn't want to waste any more of Jess's time explaining her boring life, "So how about you show me around so I can buy a ton of furniture I can't even use right now?" She asked Jess.

Laughing, Jess stood up, and motioned for Aubrey to go first, "Got it, just lead the way."


Later on, Aubrey couldn't believe she'd spent almost two hours at the store, going over decorating schemes, fabric choices, and wood colors with Jess.

She closed the place down and left with spending a small fortune, and pictures so she could see if the pieces she picked would go with the overall feel of her house. Jess agreed that they wouldn't deliver any furniture until Aubrey called her to say it was okay.

Although, this was kind of premature since she really should be renovating before decorating, but Aubrey felt so good. She wasn't sure if it was because she ran into Jess and therefore felt another connection to her hometown.

Driving back into Burlington, Aubrey made one more stop at Walmart to pick up some toiletries, towels, a shower curtain, and a blow up mattress, along with bedding.

As she meandered down the aisles of the bedding area, Aubrey thought about what her friend told her. Three kids! It was hard to fathom for Aubrey. Her children were her books. She'd been fortunate to publish ten so far, with a contract for a series of three more.

Jess told her how proud everyone here was that one of their own had made it big in California. She also informed Aubrey that she was still in touch with a few people from high school and promised to get everyone together soon.

Aubrey smiled, picked up a set of single sheets for her blow-up mattress, and sighed for the pitifulness of her situation.

As she was driving back down Milwaukee Avenue, Aubrey decided that she didn't want to go back to a big, empty house just yet. A last minute decision had her pulling into the parking lot across from the theater.

She crossed the street, laughing as she dodged cars, and scanned the schedule. There was a movie that was starting in less than twenty minutes, so she bought a ticket and went inside.

The place looked absolutely nothing like it did when she was in school. They were just starting the renovations when she'd run off to college, and the differences were amazing.

She chose a romantic comedy because she wanted to laugh, bought her ticket, and got her snacks.

The movie she chose was in the main theater so Aubrey went inside, and was flooded with memories. Even though the walls and floors were different, the ornate ceiling was left relatively untouched. It was like being torn between two times, and Aubrey wasn't sure how that made her feel yet.

Someone said, "Excuse me," and moved past her in the aisle. Moving to let the stranger pass by, Aubrey caught a quick glance at a very nice butt, and smiled.

Maybe it was all that describing in her books, but Aubrey had some very complimentary adjectives regarding the stranger's derriere.

Luckily, the previews started, and she was forced to look up at the screen, and not at the man's body parts.

The movie was funny, and Aubrey was thankful for that. She needed the distraction of something other than her own thoughts for a while.

As the theater lights came up, she looked over and noticed the stranger with the sexy rear was looking at her. Never one to shy from such a look, she looked right back at him. Finally, he nodded, and got up to leave. Aubrey giggled and watched him go. She tended to put men off with her straightforwardness. Still not sure if that trait was a virtue, or a curse, she shrugged and left the theater.

"Did you like what you saw?" The question came from behind Aubrey as she exited the theater.

Turning around, and seeing the stranger in her row, she retorted, "I did, thank you. Very interesting."

He gave her the strangest look because she was pretty sure he wasn't sure if she was talking about the movie or him, and held the door for her to go outside.

Aubrey said, "Thanks," and went out to get into her car.

# Chapter 4

The house was dark when Aubrey pulled into the driveway. She cursed at herself for forgetting to leave a light on. Geez!

Walking around the back of the house, Aubrey was glad that the porch light from her neighbor's house cast enough light that she could at least get inside. Flipping on switches as she went, Aubrey had the entire first floor lit up within minutes.

She went back out to get her new purchases, and brought them inside.

It took her a little bit to get the bed out of the box and inflated, the new sheets really should be washed before she used them, but no one but her would know, so she just put them on the bed and went upstairs to clean up.

Even the act of taking a shower was work since she had to put up the shower curtain, and get her toiletries situated.

"Well, you just had to be all about doing it yourself," She said to herself sarcastically as she stepped into the shower. Pride was a funny thing sometimes.

Her mind wandered as she showered, wondering if she should take a different tact with her new leading lady. She was a detective and was sexy as hell while being brilliant; things every woman possessed in Aubrey's mind.

After her shower, Aubrey quickly blow dried her hair, brushed her teeth, and put on her face cream. Even the act of having to put on, what she referred to as "old lady cream" left her with a scowl on her face.

She went downstairs, and got herself tucked into bed, at the back end of the living room. Since most of the renovations would take place in the master suite, it didn't seem reasonable to sleep upstairs where there would most certainly be a mess.

Plugging in her phone, she checked it, and saw she'd missed a couple of calls from friends, and decided to just return them tomorrow. She was beat from all of today's events.

As she drifted off to sleep, Aubrey thought for sure she heard a woman's voice singing. It was very distant, but it sounded like a lullaby.


The next morning, Aubrey woke up to the sound of knocking. Panic flooded her chest because she'd forgotten where she was. The knocking persisted, and she yelled out, "Just a minute!"

Getting up, Aubrey looked around, the room flooded with sunlight, and wondered how late it was.

She walked over to the front door, and saw it was her dad. With a smile, Aubrey opened the door, and said, "Good morning."

Greg's smile faded when he saw his daughter, "My Lord, what happened?" He asked, and rushed inside.

Confused by her father's words, and the look on his face, Aubrey turned around and went into the kitchen. "I'm fine, Dad," She looked back at him, "What do you think is wrong?"

Putting down the cups of coffee and donuts on the counter, Greg turned and took his daughter into his arms. "I'm sorry I scared you, it's just when I saw the tears in your eyes; I assumed something happened."

"Tears?" Aubrey asked him, and went to retrieve her phone. She turned on the camera, then reversed it so she could see herself. Sure enough, her eyes were puffy, as if she'd been crying for hours. She looked back up at her dad, and said, "I have no idea why I look like this."

Slipping into doctor mode, Greg stepped forward and ran his hand over his daughter's temple, then checked her pulse. Seeing that everything seemed normal, he started to relax. "I'm sorry, sweetheart."

Shrugging, Aubrey answered, "No reason to be, Dad, I'm not sure what the deal is. I must have had a bad dream that I can't remember."

Checking his watch, Greg nodded, and said, "Well, you should probably get dressed, Cole will be here in a few minutes."

Aubrey took a quick sip of her coffee, nodded, and went upstairs to get dressed.

She was just putting on her clothes when she heard the front doorbell ring. Listening for a couple of seconds, she heard her dad answer it, and went back to pulling her long, dark brown hair back into a pony tail.

Coming down stairs a few minutes later, Aubrey felt much better. Since it was a "work" day, she chose an old, but very comfy pair of shorts, along with one of her UCLA t-shirts. Her feet were bare, and with her hair pulled back, she looked much younger than her thirty-two years.

She practically ran into the kitchen, and stopped dead when she saw who her father was talking to in her kitchen. It was "great butt guy!" Shaking herself mentally, to get her mind on track, Aubrey pasted on her business smile and greeted her guest, "Good morning." She noticed that he gave a quick look of surprise before covering it up with his own game face.

Cole Rafferty had seen pictures of Aubrey Slojankonkowski at her parents' house and on the backs of her books, but none of that could do her justice. "Good morning," He returned, and held his hand out to shake hers. "I'm Cole Rafferty."

Although Aubrey was thinking, "hunky leading man name," she said, "Hi, I'm Aubrey."

Challenging her a bit, Cole asked, "Or should I call you A.J?"

He was good, she'd give him that. "No, I think Aubrey is fine for now."

Cole nodded, and turned to grab his pad of paper and pen off the kitchen counter. "I'm ready whenever you are," He said.

She liked that he was alright with getting down to business, Aubrey led the way back through the front of the house, and into the living room. Slightly cringing at the sight of her blow up mattress and pile of clothes, she tried to be professional. "I'd like just a face lift here, new paint, new flooring, to check and make sure the fireplace is safe, and then a new mantle."

He nodded, and took notes, without saying anything. They went back through the dining room, with Aubrey explaining that she would be doing some of the work in that room, and what she would need him to do.

Cole followed Aubrey, and her father, and was blown away. She was most definitely a woman who knew her own mind.

They went into the kitchen, discussed countertops and flooring for a few minutes, then went on into the breakfast nook.

As they got to the closet with only a toilet in it, Cole asked, "Do you want me to take this out?"

Aubrey laughed, but said, "No, it might come in handy during renovations, but we'll have to put a light of some form in there."

The three of them went downstairs to the basement. Aubrey asked Cole, "What do you think we should do down here?"

After looking through the family room, the bedroom, and bathroom, Cole replied, "Not much, new flooring in the family room, maybe a fresh coat of paint. I know the company that did the renovations a few years ago, and their work is solid."

She appreciated his honesty, and the fact that he did his homework. "Okay, sounds good," She replied, and they went back upstairs to the main level.

As they walked through the kitchen, Aubrey stopped, "I need food," She said, and grabbed a donut out of the box on their way through the room.

They went upstairs, to the second floor, and started in the first room they came to. It was small, with wood flooring.

Aubrey loved this room for some reason she couldn't explain. "I don't want to change anything here, except the color on the walls. The floor should stay wood, I'll just find a nice area rug."

Cole nodded, and then smiled when he saw she had chocolate smeared at the corner of her mouth. They were standing in the room, with Aubrey telling her dad that she wanted to use this room as her office.

Not thinking about what he was doing, he just reached up and used his finger to wipe off the chocolate. It was only after Aubrey stood stock still, and silent, that he realized what he'd done. "Oh, sorry, you had chocolate on your lip," He explained.

Greg was in the room, but didn't think either his daughter, or Cole, noticed. "Uh, well," He broke the silence, "let's continue."

Aubrey could only nod at her dad. Her lip still tingled from where Cole Rafferty had touched it with his thumb. Hell, they were completely dressed and her dad was in the room, but she felt like it was the most intimate encounter she'd had in some time.

They went into the next room, and Aubrey sighed, before asking, "What is it with paneling?"

Cole laughed at her question. "Some people think it looks nice," He answered, then read aloud, "No paneling," as he wrote the words on his notepad.

Shaking her head, Aubrey laughed. "Yes, and let's get rid of this carpet."

They went across the hall to the master bedroom.

Aubrey stood in the middle of the room, and watched Cole as he took measurements and made notes on his notepad.

"Nice space," Cole said, "But definitely not enough closet space, and no adjoining bath."

They went out onto the patio, and Cole whistled, "If this would be finished, it would be a great place to have your morning coffee."

It was if he'd plucked the words right out of Aubrey's mind. She stood on the patio, awestruck.

Finally Greg cleared his throat, and asked his daughter, "What do you think, honey?"

Being jostled from her thoughts, Aubrey only nodded. This man's uncanny ability for thinking her thoughts threw her a little, emotionally speaking. Sure, he has a great body, any woman within a two-mile radius would drool over his broad shoulders that tapered down into the sexiest pair of jeans Aubrey had ever seen.

They went back inside, and down the hall toward the pink bathroom and last bedroom.

Within a half hour, they were back downstairs in the kitchen. Greg and Cole were discussing some things, while Aubrey stood against the kitchen counter, and sipped her, now tepid, coffee and ogled the contractor.

"So," Cole said, and turned to face Aubrey, "I'll write up an estimate, and bring it by. Is tomorrow okay for you?"

Aubrey shook her head in agreement, "I think that's fine."

Greg knew his daughter was too lost in her thoughts to have an intelligent conversation, so he offered to walk Cole out. He came back a couple of minutes later, and watched his her, standing there against the counter.

There were things about your children that never seemed to change. Aubrey's ability to tune out the world and be lost in that mind of hers was something she'd done since she was a child. He imagined that it was a nice escape on some level, but could make her seem aloof or rude socially. "Hello?" He asked her.

Being shaken out of her musings, Aubrey looked up, and bit her lip. "I'm sorry, Dad," She answered him, then asked, "How long was I in la-la land?"

"Long enough for Cole to wonder if you were eccentric or insane," He answered dryly.

Throwing her head back Aubrey sighed, "Oh crap."

Her father patted her shoulder, and added, "I'm sure he thinks you're just some crazy writer from California. After all, that's what I've been telling people for years."

Giving him a glare, Aubrey offered, "I'm sure you have patients to see."

Leaning over, Greg gave his daughter a peck on the cheek, then nodded. "I do, indeed, so I'll leave you to your mind," he bowed, "and your home."

Chuckling at his clowning around, Aubrey followed him to the door, kissed his cheek, and waved as he walked the block to the hospital to do his rounds.

After closing the door behind her, Aubrey looked around. In the clear light of day, this place was most definitely the proverbial diamond in the rough.

Walking into the dining room, Aubrey decided there was no time like the present to get going. She walked to the front corner of the room, and pulled up the carpet. If anything, she was going to get this pet urine smell out of her house, and fast.

Standing in line at Reineman's True Value, a few minutes from the house, on Milwaukee Ave., Aubrey felt decidedly stupid. It had taken her fifteen minutes to get up a small patch of carpet, only to realize it was a bigger job than she thought.  There were strips of nails at the edge and she'd cut her finger on one of the nail edges.  She went over to her laptop and looked up carpet removal, only to find out she needed tools.

Now, she stood in line, with a hammer, a screwdriver, work gloves, and a Milky Way candy bar, because any manly work automatically demanded a side of chocolate to go with it.

The clerk looked at her for a few seconds, then went about ringing her up.

Aubrey experienced that a lot, someone who thought they might know her, but wasn't sure where they knew her from.  She never offered information, but answered honestly, if asked.

She smiled at the clerk, who was still eyeing her curiously, and left the hardware store with a smile on her face.  She would not let a little matter of a carpet kick her butt.

# Chapter 5

Two hours later, Aubrey was covered in sweat, and heaving the carpet off the floor. She'd managed to get half the room rolled up when she heard her mother come in the front door. "Hi, Mom," She called out, but didn't stop.

Standing in the entryway, watching her daughter fight with a carpet, Christine tried not to laugh. It was clear they wouldn't be going anywhere nice for lunch, since Aubrey looked like she'd been doing aerobics for the better part of the morning. "So, how's it going?" She asked rhetorically. She finally did laugh when Aubrey shot her a look. "I'm sorry," She said, and wished she could get a picture of this.

"I'm sorry, I got a little distracted with pulling up this carpet," Aubrey said to her mom.

Christine nodded to her daughter, "I can see this." She set her purse down on the steps leading upstairs, then walked back toward the entryway into the dining room, and leaned against the wall. "May I offer some advice?" She asked her daughter.

Standing up, and blowing her hair out of her face, Aubrey said, "Sure," sarcastically.

Ignoring her daughter's tone, just this once, Christine said, "Well, as someone who has pulled up carpet, and seen others do it, I can tell you it's easier if you cut it up first."

Looking blankly at her mother, Aubrey said, "I don't understand."

Christine put up one finger, to gesture for her daughter to "hold on," and went out to her car. When she came back in she told Aubrey, "Unroll it please."

Torn between stubbornness, and following her mother's directions, Aubrey chose the latter, and unrolled the carpet.

Holding out a cutting blade, Christine instructed Aubrey, "Now, take this and cut the carpet into three pieces," and motioned how Aubrey should do it.

Dutifully listening to her mother's directions, Aubrey did as instructed. She handed her mom back the cutting knife and asked, "What now?"

"Now," Christine pointed to the center, "Start rolling up that center row."

Doing as her mother asked, Aubrey easily rolled up a strip of carpet. When it was pushed into the kitchen, she came back into the dining room, and asked, "So, where were you when I started this?"

Laughing, Christine shrugged, and told her, "Well, you didn't tell me you were pulling up carpet."

Nodding, Aubrey answered, "That's true." She asked her mom, "What's for lunch?"

"How about," Christine started, "I go out and get us some sub sandwiches that we can eat here, and you just continue on with your job here?" She pointed at the carpet.

Aubrey nodded, relieved that her mom was so accommodating. She nodded, and answered, "Thanks."

Smiling, Christine grabbed her purse, and left her daughter to her chore.

When her mother returned, half an hour later, Aubrey had already gotten the second strip of carpet up and out the back door, along with the first piece.

"Nice job," Christine said to her daughter as they sat down on the window seat in the breakfast nook.

Taking a bite out of her sandwich, Aubrey nodded, and said, "Thanks."

Watching her daughter, Christine took a bite of her sandwich and waited for a few minutes before asking, "So what did you think of Cole?"

Recognizing the tone of her mother's question, Aubrey knew that her dad had already given her a full report on the "Cole situation." She slowly chewed the bite of sandwich she had in her mouth, and contemplated the answer she wanted to give. Finally, she said, "Well, he seems to have the same thoughts as I do for this place, so that's good."

Christine gave her daughter the, "you don't fool me," look.

Aubrey rolled her eyes, then answered, "Okay, he's hot! Is that what you want to hear?" She asked.

Smiling, Christine took a bite of her own sandwich, chewed it, and then responded, "Maybe."

Laughing, they continued to eat, and talk about other things.

Aubrey asked her mom about a couple of the local foundations she was involved in, and was pleased to hear about the progress. That was something her parents taught her from a young age, "You always help someone when you can." It was a motto she chose to follow throughout her adulthood, but in California, she was always giving at a distance, to some charity she never visited or saw. Here, she was able to not only contribute time and resources, but she could also do it with her mom, and that made Aubrey want to help more.

As she walked her mother out to her car, she waved at her neighbor, next door.

"Okay, so dinner tomorrow night?" Christine asked her daughter.

Using her hands to make a cross on her chest, Aubrey replied, "Cross my heart, I promise."

Even knowing her daughter was incorrigible, Christine still marveled at the trait. Surely their daughter inherited such a quality from Greg, and not her. "Bye," She said, and kissed Aubrey before heading off to a meeting at the hospital.

When Aubrey came back inside, she stood in the doorway of the dining room, and said, "So, we meet again," to the carpet. "You shall not win, not this time," She said aloud and went back to work.

Several hours later, Aubrey was still in the dining room. Getting the carpet up was actually the easy part, now she was scraping up the padding that was stuck to the wood floor beneath, probably due to the pet urine.

As she got the last of the nasty padding up, she decided to take a break from her work and check her emails.

She walked into the kitchen, grabbed a bottled water, and turned on her laptop. Deciding she wanted to procrastinate on the work front, she checked her personal email first. There were a few short ones from friends, telling her they missed her. She returned them all, feeling that friendships were like plants, they needed to be attended to in order to grow.

Once she opened up her professional email, she sighed. There were no less than a dozen emails from her editor regarding her current book. Two from her agent, since she knew that Aubrey wouldn't answer the phone for several days. There was one from her publicist, and that one made her laugh since her publicist HATED using email.

Before she'd left California, she'd sat down with her "team" and explained that she needed a week without interrupting phone calls and the normal harassment that goes along with being a successful novelist. They looked at her like she'd gone mad, but Aubrey was adamant about needing the time.

Sending back brief replies, she felt that she'd done due diligence on the work front.

Going back into the dining room, Aubrey decided to take out her frustration on the nail strips that ran along the edges of the room. She turned around, grabbed the hammer off the counter, and went back to work.

The next time she looked up, Aubrey noticed that the sun was starting to dip low in the sky. The shadows ran long across the floor, and her stomach was grumbling.

She stood up, and stretched her back. The muscles were sore from all the bending and pulling, but she'd felt good doing the physical labor.

Remembering that she needed to call the cable company so she could have internet access, she grabbed her cell phone off of the counter to make the phone call.

As soon as she'd hung up, her phone started ringing, so she pressed connect, "Hello," she answered, not recognizing the number.

"Ms. Slojankonkowski?" Cole Rafferty asked when she answered. Her voice sounded breathy, and he didn't like what the sound of it did to his insides.

Aubrey, feeling a little leery, gave a quiet, "Yes," as an answer.

Getting his impulses under control, Cole said, "This is Cole Rafferty, the contractor, from this morning."

"Oh, yes," Aubrey replied, and made a mental note to add his name into her phone contacts.

Cole wasn't supposed to meet with her until tomorrow, but he'd been thinking about her almost non-stop since this morning, and so he called. "I wanted to know if you wanted to have a dinner meeting tonight instead of meeting up tomorrow morning."

His suggestion gave Aubrey pause. She cocked her head, and asked him, "Is this a meeting, or dinner?"

She was quick, Cole would give her that. Perhaps that's what fascinated him so much about her. "Your choice," He returned.

Hmmm, Aubrey pondered the proposal for a full minute. She wasn't sure what to make of this Cole Rafferty, but she liked the way his words made her feel. "How about dinner, tonight, and business tomorrow?" She asked him.

"Sounds great, I'll be there in a half hour," Cole answered then hung up.

Standing in her kitchen, Aubrey stared at her phone. She couldn't really get a handle on this guy, and that both excited her and made her nervous. Glancing at the time, she ran upstairs to shower.

Thirty minutes later, on the dot, Cole Rafferty rang the doorbell. He could see Aubrey come down the stairs through the narrow windows that flanked the front door. She was practically floating down them, in a dress that made her look very feminine. His nerves started roiling around in his stomach when she opened the door.

"Hi," Aubrey said, a little breathless from rushing around to get ready.

He noticed that her long, wavy hair was piled up on her head, and Cole only wanted to free it from the confines of whatever held it in place. He wanted to kiss her lips that were rosy pink from the lip gloss she wore, and he wanted to feel her arms around him. Instead, he just gave her a throaty, "Hi."

It was tough for Aubrey not to laugh when he suddenly looked so nervous. She was too, but for an entirely different reason. He was gorgeous! Dressed in khaki pants, and a polo shirt, Cole looked like he'd just walked off a photo shoot for GQ magazine. If she thought he looked good in jeans and a t-shirt, now he just blew her away. Her body tingled with awareness and she loved it. "Are you nervous, Cole?" She asked him, baiting him a bit.

Cole was not oblivious to the mental games women could play, although with Aubrey, he felt more like it was an experiment rather than teasing. "Yes," He answered her honestly, "You're beautiful."

The words silenced Aubrey. She wasn't expecting to hear the sincerity, and heat they produced. "Thank you, you are very handsome yourself," She said, and grabbed her bag off the little table next to the door. "Should we go?"

They walked out into the cool, spring evening. Aubrey was glad she'd grabbed a shrug to wear over her dress, and slipped it on as they walked.

Watching her put on her sweater, Cole was intrigued. She was naturally graceful with her slim build, and seemed to do everything with purpose. He planned to take a good look inside that head of hers tonight, and hoped he enjoyed it as much as he anticipated.

He opened the door, and waited for her to get into his sedan, before walking around to the driver's side.

"No truck tonight?" Aubrey asked him.

Cole shook his head, "Nope, I'm a grown up tonight."

Looking straight ahead, Aubrey sighed, and said, "Pity."

Her quick wit made Cole laugh. It had been a long time since he'd been with someone so sophisticated. Not saying that the women here in Burlington weren't sophisticated, just that he hadn't had time to look for someone who matched him in that department. "Hope you like local food?" He asked her as they turned onto Randolph Street and then made a left onto W. State Street.

Aubrey didn't answer him, only watched as they passed St. Mary's Catholic Church on the left. It was still a stunning building to look at. When Cole pulled into a parking lot across the street from the church, she shot him a questioning look.

Cole got out of the car, and came around to open up her door. He didn't miss the look on her face. Sometimes you just needed to surprise a woman.

Without saying anything, Cole led her to the sidewalk, and they crossed McHenry Street.

When Aubrey realized they were going into a local place called, B.J. Wentker's, she smiled. She hadn't been in here since they renovated it years earlier. A few of her friends had praised it over the years on Facebook, and her parents went there every now and again, so she knew it had to be nice.

As Cole held the door for her to enter, Aubrey felt as if she'd been thrown back into a different century. The place was redone to look as it had a hundred years ago. "Wow," Was all she said, as Cole led her over to a table.

"I know, right?" He said as he sat down across from her. Looking around, he smiled at the bartender, who was a friend, and commented, "I love the architecture."

Aubrey looked over at him, and knew his words were a reflection of her own. "Yes, something about it makes me feel......almost romantic."

His eyebrows raised, Cole returned, "Well then, I'll remember to bring you here more often."

She couldn't help it, his words made her laugh. Aubrey loved someone with a good sense of humor and quick tongue. Of course, she wouldn't mind if his tongue held other secrets too. She hushed herself mentally. There was no need to go down that erotic, mental road just yet.

## Chapter 6

The bartender hollered over to Cole, "Hey, what'll it be tonight?"

Looking at Aubrey, Cole waited.

"I'll have an Amaretto Stone Sour, blended please," She told Cole, and smiled, as he stood to walk over to the bar.

Aubrey hadn't had one of those since the last time she came home because no one in California seemed to know how to make them right. She watched Cole, as he shook hands with the bartender, who looked strangely familiar, and chatted while her drink was being made.

A nice young woman came up to their table and said, "Good evening," she handed Aubrey a menu, and placed one at Cole's place. "Is there anything I can start you off with?" She asked Aubrey.

Shaking her head no, Aubrey smiled, and finally looked down at the menu.

She was still trying to decide on what she wanted to eat when Cole returned with their drinks. He placed hers down, then sat and took a sip of his beer.

At Aubrey's look, he offered, "I'm only having one with dinner," he winked, "I'm not in the habit of drinking and driving."

And there it was again, Aubrey thought to herself, his ability to know exactly what she was thinking. It was unnerving and thrilling all bundled up into a ball inside her. "I suspected as much," She countered, trying not to show him her true feelings just yet.

"Okay, let's get down to it then," Cole started, "How does a girl from small town Wisconsin end up being a famous murder/mystery writer?"

After taking a healthy sip of her drink, Aubrey smiled, and answered, "Well, I've been a dramatic story teller all my life, or so my parents keep telling me."

Cole nodded, and said, "I can see that."

Surprised, Aubrey asked him, "Really? How's that?"

Oh now he'd put himself in the hot seat. "Well," Cole began, "I see your mind working constantly. You like a good conversation, and a girly drink," he pointed to her glass, "and I think you know your own mind very well."

All of his observations were true, Aubrey had to admit. "And?" She asked him, wanting to know what he truly thought.

"And, I'll bet if I gave you just a thread of information, you'd have no problem whatsoever coming up with some story that would have the whole room entranced." He leaned forward, "And you've already got me entranced."

Having no idea if it was the drink, or Cole's words, Aubrey found herself sinking into a well of something similar to comfort. She was warm, and felt a sort of connection to him that she couldn't describe. Trying to turn the conversation, she asked him, "Have you read my books?"

Cole had to laugh. "Oh yes, ma'am." He tried to ease the look of discomfort she wore. "It's not meant to mock you, you're a brilliant writer," He said, then added, "It's just that your mother is a huge supporter and had one of your books in my hand about ten minutes after I met her."

Now it was Aubrey's turn to laugh. "That, doesn't surprise me," She answered. "I'm sorry if she shoved it on you."

"It was my pleasure," Cole answered, the tone in his voice low and intimate.

Aubrey was about to say something else when their waitress came over to take their orders. They both ordered steak, and waited for her to leave to continue their conversation.

Cole took another drink of his beer, and told her, "What surprised me the most, was the details, you know, the insight into the criminal mind." He gave her a cautious look, and asked her, "You don't have bodies buried out in some deserted lot in California, do you?"

That had Aubrey chuckling. "No, but thanks for asking." She tilted her head a little, and told him, "I spent hours, days, and weeks interviewing real detectives and in libraries researching that stuff."

"Does it ever depress you?" Cole asked her. "You know, the murder and mayhem?"

Aubrey took a moment to think about the question. She'd actually never been asked that before. "No," She finally answered, "It's more of just a side effect, if you will, the real thrill for me is solving the puzzle."

Cole studied her as she spoke, then added, "I can see that."

Leaning forward herself, she rested her chin on her hands, and asked him, "How do you see that?"

The conversation was quickly turning into the murky area of intimacy again, and yet, Cole didn't feel as if he should hold back, not with Aubrey. "I see that you want justice, and you get it," Then he went on to say, "And I see that you want your women to be all things, sexy, strong, empathetic, but tough enough to take the bullshit men sometimes dish out."

Now Aubrey leaned back, a smile on her face. "Mr. Rafferty, I think you just earned a lot of brownie points."

She wanted to say more, but their food arrived.

As they ate, the conversation darted to various subjects. The changes in Burlington were a big part of it. Aubrey explained to him that when she was a kid, they would allow ice skating on Echo Lake, and she would go sledding down the "water tower hill."

Cole listened to her talk. He was fascinated by her description of things. No wonder she was a successful writer, it was just natural for her to set the scene. He sensed a bit of feeling lost though, and that was something he didn't expect from her.

"Now, your turn," Aubrey said to him, "I don't think you grew up around here, I'd have seen you." She winked, and said, "I'm guessing you're only a few years older than I am and I would've dated you, or one of my friends would have."

Blushing, Cole took another sip of his beer. "I'm not from around here," Was his answer.

Expecting more of an explanation, Aubrey waited.

Sighing, Cole offered, "I grew up just outside of Chicago, in a not-so-small town. Went to college for Contracting, and fix up people's houses." He shrugged, "Pretty boring, I guess."

Aubrey shook her head, "Oh, you underestimate yourself, Mr. Rafferty," she said his name slowly, drawing it out. "Why did you pick Burlington?" She asked him.

Easy answer, so Cole told her, "A friend of mine was thinking about retiring, and we'd talked about me taking over his business." He leaned back, and smiled at someone he recognized at the bar, before adding, "It was just the right timing."

"And how do you know my parents?" She asked him.

Cole was surprised by that question, but responded quickly, "When you're parents bought their place out on Hwy W, it needed a whole lot of updating."

Doing the calculations in her head, Aubrey realized he'd known her parents for four years. Then she wondered why her mother hadn't brought him up sooner, and made a mental note to ask her mother that tomorrow night at dinner. "I see," She said to Cole, then asked him, "and would you say you're friends with them?"

Confused by the tone in her question, Cole answered, "Yes," then asked her, "How come I feel like I'm being interrogated here?"

Aubrey was ashamed of herself. He was right and this wasn't one of her novels where the cop gets the answers. "I'm sorry," She said to him. "I'm just wondering how it is that we've not met before now."

That statement was one that Cole wondered about himself. "When were you home last?" He asked her.

More calculations were involved before Aubrey answered him with, "It's been at least five years."

"And that's why," He countered.

Retreating mentally, Aubrey was feeling the sting of shame as she sat there. She hadn't been back to see her parents in over five years. That was shocking when she thought about it. Her parents had come out to see her the last three years, but she hadn't given it any thought.

Cole watched her, and knew she was berating herself for not being here more. "Hey," He said, and reached across to tip her chin upward with his fingers, "No regrets, your life is your own."

When Cole put it like that, she felt better. "I guess, I just know that my parents did a lot to support my dream, and maybe I put them off to pursue it."

"From what I've seen, and our conversations," Cole told her, "I don't see that they feel that way." He smiled, and dropped his hand from her chin, "I'd say they are about the proudest parents on the face of the earth."

Aubrey blushed. "Thank you," She said softly.

Cole motioned for the check. "I'd offer you dessert, they have some great stuff, but I'd rather do something different."

His cryptic words made Aubrey smile. "Okay," She said and waited for him to finish up with the bill. It was on her mind to offer to split the bill, but that would have probably ticked him off.

As they walked across the street, to where his car was parked, Aubrey asked him, "Would you have been offended if I offered to pay for my own dinner?"

Giving her a fierce look, Cole answered, "Hell, yes!"

His emotion, made her stop walking. "Really?" She asked him.

Cole stopped too, and faced her on the sidewalk. "Not to be rude, but when I invite a lady out to dinner, big time author or not, I'm paying."

Well, Aubrey thought to herself, he just put me in my place. She didn't say anything else, just nodded once, and began walking again.

They got into the car, and didn't say anything during the short drive toward downtown.

As soon as they pulled up next to the park, Aubrey knew where he was taking her, and she smiled. "Adrian's, I should have known," She said on the trail of a laugh.

Relief poured over him. He thought that his macho attitude after they'd left the restaurant might have upset her. He turned off the car, and turned to her, the only light cast by street lamps at the edge of the parking lot, so her face was in partial shadow. He asked her, "Did I tick you off?"

Aubrey wouldn't pretend to not know what he was talking about. "Not at all," She answered, "You had a valid point, and I was just curious." Then she commented, "I'm not sure how to take the "big time author" title, but I'm pretty sure you didn't mean it as a dig."

They sat there, in his car, with the quiet of the evening enveloping them. Even though he shouldn't go on, Cole said, "You intrigue me, I'm intimidated by your success, even though you don't flaunt it, and even though I'm a success in my own right."

Once again, Aubrey was firmly put in her place. "Well then," She started, "Back at you," and opened her car door to get out before she kissed him.

They crossed Milwaukee Ave. and Aubrey started to get excited as they came up to the window at Adrian's Frozen Custard. Only open seasonally, Adrian's was a Burlington staple. Even though Aubrey perused the menu, she knew she wouldn't order any of it.

When it was their turn, she walked up, smiled at the clerk, and asked, "Can I have a medium twist cone please?"

She stepped away so Cole could order, and sought out a newly vacated place at one of the metal picnic tables in front of the parlor.

Cole joined her, a funny look on his face.

"What?" She asked him.

After sitting, Cole asked her, "With all those selections, you just wanted a twist cone?"

Aubrey gave him a dry look, and replied, "You simply don't mess with a classic, Cole."

The combination of her words, her tone, and the look on her face made Cole laugh. She was complete puzzle to him, with so many facets that he was pretty sure a lifetime wouldn't be enough time to figure them all out.

He stood up to go over and get their order, while Aubrey stayed put, to save their coveted seats. It was a Wednesday night, but even being a weeknight the crowds couldn't stay away from Adrian's.

When Cole handed her the cone, she took a long lick of it, and sighed. There was nothing in the world that tasted like Adrian's frozen custard.

Even though he had his own dessert, Cole focused more on watching Aubrey enjoying hers than eating his. Perhaps it was the neat way in which she held the cone, as if she had to make sure none of the delicious dessert dripped. Maybe it was the way she dabbed at her mouth, as if she was afraid of making a mess. His thoughts flew back to the morning, when he'd been bold and wiped the chocolate off the edge of her lips.

When Aubrey came up for air, instead of drowning herself in the delicious sweetness of the frozen custard, she realized that Cole was watching her. The look he wore was voracious. The fact that she wasn't sure if it was the dessert or her he was ravenous about, made her stomach tighten.

"Cole?" A voice asked from behind them, making both Cole and Aubrey turn around to see who was talking.

Cole recognized a friend of his. Her name was Linda, and she'd asked him out a few times before. He'd always begged it off but earlier in the week, he'd finally agreed. They were due to go out on Friday night. And seeing the look that Linda was giving Aubrey, he already wanted to back out of the commitment.

Aubrey watched the interplay between the woman and Cole and she was just sitting back and studying them. Cole looked very uncomfortable, while the woman looked pissed off, and Aubrey was pretty sure she was the reason for it.

"Hi, Linda," Cole said quietly. He turned to Aubrey, and introduced her, "Linda, this is Aubrey," he smiled, "Aubrey, this is Linda."

Linda gave Aubrey a look of disinterest, but nodded. Aubrey figured that if the other woman wanted to be rude, then she had no obligation to be friendly, and only nodded herself in response.

Someone called Linda away, so she smiled at Cole, completely ignoring Aubrey.

They finished up their frozen custard a few minutes later, and made their way back to Cole's car. "Hey," Aubrey said to him, trying to lighten the mood, "You can't help it if you've got women fighting over you."

Her read on the situation made him feel at ease. "I'm sorry," He responded, "She's a nice person, or at least I thought so."

Feeling obligated, Aubrey stopped and faced him, saying, "Women are possessive over two things, Cole. Clothes, and men."

When she put it like that, Cole actually felt like he might understand the opposite sex a little better. "I'll remember that," He said as he opened up the car door for her.

## Chapter 7

They pulled into the driveway of Aubrey's house, and sat for a few minutes. The awkwardness caused by Linda was gone. As Cole got out, he asked her, "So what's your take on movies?"

Aubrey got out of the car, and answered, "Funny, sad, action," she winked, "anything as long as it transports me out of my real life." She wondered if he knew that she was the one near him at the movie theater the other night.

"Politics?" Cole asked as they walked around the front of the house.

Shocked, Aubrey gasped, "Cole Rafferty, on a first date you're asking about politics," she pretended to be taken aback, "why don't you just ask my age and sexual preference?" She asked him jokingly.

Cole turned her around, pinning her to the front door. "I think," He started to lean in, "I don't care about your age or political preferences," his lips were only inches from hers, "but I'm pretty sure I know your sexual preference," and he kissed her.

The kiss swept Aubrey up into a maelstrom of craziness. His lips were everywhere, on her neck, her lips, and even her ear lobes. It was like he was memorizing her with them, and causing her insides to puddle up into need.

She, of course, returned his eager kisses with her own, she was a woman who knew what she wanted, after all.

When his lips met hers again, she upped the ante and opened her mouth to deepen it. The growl she heard from him, confirmed that he was as moved by the kiss as she was.

Cole felt like he was climbing inside of her, his arms were around her like vise grips. Her mouth was hot, and as eager as his. There was no "taking over" where Aubrey was concerned, it was completely mutual. He'd never had a woman make him feel that way before. Finally, he had to come up for air, and stepped back.

"Wow," Aubrey sighed, as Cole released her.

Smiling, Cole looked at her, and wanted to continue where they left off.

Since Aubrey was smart enough to know where this would lead, if she allowed it, she decided to be honest. "I'd invite you in, but I don't sleep with men, even the hot contractor ones, on a first date."

Leave it to her to be honest and give him an out. "I appreciate your honesty," he said, "and I'll take the hot contractor comment as a compliment."

"You should," Aubrey answered. "Now, go, before I change my mind and I let you inside to see my single blow up mattress."

Laughing again, Cole nodded. "Duly noted," He replied. "How about dinner tomorrow?" He asked her as he walked backward down her front walk.

"I'm having dinner with my parents, but you're more than welcome to join us," She gave him a wink, "since you're already friends."

She laid it right out there for him, and Cole admired that about her. "Friends, it is," He stopped and pointed to her, "For now."

Biting her bottom lip, Aubrey returned, "For now," and turned to go inside.

Aubrey leaned against the front door and listened for the sound of Cole's car leaving. When she heard the hum of it going down the street, she took a deep breath. That man packed a wallop to her libido. Everything inside her ached, actually ached, for him. She couldn't remember having that strong of a reaction to anyone.

She started to walk into the entryway, and missed placing her purse on the table near the door, so the purse fell onto the floor with a loud thump.

Rolling her eyes, Aubrey reached down and picked up her bag. To her surprise, when she picked it up, it snagged on one of the floor boards, actually lifting it up a bit.

"Another thing for Cole to fix," She mumbled and put the purse safely onto the table. She made sure the doors were all locked up, once again turning on all the lights on the first floor, as she went. There was something a little eerie about being in such a big house by yourself.

Later, as she was drifting off to sleep, the sensuous thoughts of Cole's kiss were replaced with the sounds of a woman crying.


The next morning, Aubrey woke up, and felt exhausted. Looking at her phone, she saw that she'd slept a solid eight hours, which was awesome, but she felt like she'd just slept for minutes. Reaching up, she found tears in her eyes again, and wondered why she would cry in her sleep.

Did it have to do with being back in her hometown? Was she worried that she wouldn't be able to write here? Whatever the reason was, Aubrey knew she needed some decent sleep if she was going to make a go of this. She made a mental note to ask her dad about it when she went over to their place for dinner later.

It was still early, but she'd decided to meet with Cole at eight for a breakfast meeting. She knew it was just an excuse to be with him, but she couldn't help it, there was something about him that drew her in.

At 7:45am, Aubrey was just coming down the stairs, when she saw Cole walking up to the door. A smile planted firmly on her face, she walked over and opened the door just as he was about to knock. "Good morning," She greeted him.

Cole smiled, then let it fade. "Are you alright?" He asked, concerned. She looked exhausted.

"I know," Aubrey offered before he could ask anything else, "I looked this way yesterday too."

Coming inside, Cole asked her, "Are you just not sleeping well here?"

Aubrey sighed, and shook her head in denial, "I was out within an hour of you dropping me off last night. I'm just not sure what's going on." She led the way into the kitchen to grab her phone and thought he'd followed her, but when she'd turned around, Cole was standing at the entryway of the dining room, and looked surprised. "Oh, yeah," I pulled up that nasty carpet yesterday," She told him.

Smiling, Cole replied, "So I see, well don't do too much, he-woman, my crew won't have anything left to do when they start."

She sauntered over to where he stood, and ran a hand down his arm, loving the way the muscles quivered as her fingers moved along them. "So, you're relatively confident I'm going to hire you for this job?" She asked him.

Up until that moment, Cole would have said yes. "Uh, not now," He said instead.

Aubrey winked at him, "Well, take me to breakfast and schmooze me into hiring you."

After a couple of seconds, he winked, and answered, "Okay."

They took his truck this morning, and Aubrey was surprised at how clean it was for a work truck. She said as much, and received a stern look for it. "I'm a clean guy," Was all he said.

Driving downtown, Aubrey took note of the park near the library. It used to have a large water fountain that she played near as a kid, but now that was gone.

Cole took her to the family style restaurant off of Hwy 36. She smiled, and followed him inside.

They were being shown to their table by the hostess when Aubrey turned to him and said, "I worked here for one day when I was fifteen."

"Really?" Cole asked her with a smile, as they sat down in their booth.

She nodded her thanks to the hostess, then turned back to him, and explained, "It was called something else back then," she smiled as she looked down at the menu, "let's just say that the food service industry and I didn't see eye to eye."

Cole laughed, "I'll bet." He looked down at his own menu, "My first job was coming up to my uncle's farm out by Lake Geneva, and working it."

Impressed, Aubrey replied, "Nice."

Shaking his head, Cole said, "No, it was dirty, even dirtier than what I do now."

She could see that. Aubrey tried to decide what she wanted to eat, but her feelings of giddiness at being with Cole messed with her appetite. "Thank you for last night," She said to him, over the top of her menu.

Her tone, no longer playful, got his attention. As his eyes met hers, the atmosphere around them ignited. "You're very welcome," He answered in the same slow tone.

The server set down glasses of water, and Aubrey wondered if she should've just poured them over their heads, it might've cooled them both down. Instead, she just smiled until the server left. "Okay, before we get all tangled up with what's between us, why don't we get business out of the way?" She asked Cole.

With a woman as intuitive as Aubrey was, Cole knew she'd never leave him wondering too long about what she was thinking. "Okay," He answered, and pulled out his portfolio. He handed it to her, and took out the copy he would keep for himself.

"Do you want me to go over it with you, or do you want to read it yourself, then ask questions?" He asked her.

It was surprising to see the quote done up in such a professional, and easy-to-understand way. He listed all the anticipated costs, per room, and then added some upgrades she could choose from.

After a quick look, she asked a few questions, and then they placed their orders.

Cole wasn't sure what she was thinking, so he asked her, "Is it good?"

Putting down the portfolio, Aubrey answered, "Honestly, it looks great, and you've been meticulous, which I appreciate. I don't have any reference as far as price goes, that would be something my mom would know better, but I'm fine with it."

Surprised that he'd been worried, Cole tried to redeem himself, and commented, "I want to work with you."

Smiling at him, Aubrey countered, "I think we both know what we both want to do."

Even this early in the morning, she wasn't going to pull punches. "How do you do it?" He asked her.

"Do what?" Aubrey asked him back.

Cole cocked his head just a bit, and studied her, before answering, "Be this straightforward, without coming off as pompous or rude."

She had to consider his words for a few moments before responding with, "In California, I had to be ruthless, to the point of rudeness, but just in the beginning. Then, once I started to find some success, well, I'm me, why be anything different?"

Nodding, Cole respected that perspective.

"My parents always knew I sort of marched to the beat of my own drum," She smiled, "and they let me be that way."

Being bold, Cole reached across the table and wrapped his fingers around Aubrey's. As soon as their fingers were connected, a shot of arousal went through him.

In an unexpected move, Aubrey leaned forward, and kiss his fingers before releasing them. At his look, she said, "Work first, and then play."

He nodded, and pulled his hand back to his side. "Okay, sorry."

Aubrey winked at him, to let him know it was okay. "Now, do I just pay you with a check, or cash?"

It amazed Cole that she could stay on task, he'd long forgotten about the work part. "Oh, uh," He picked up his portfolio, "Just turn to the last page, and read over the contract, I usually ask for half in advance, and then, if you're happy with the work, the balance at the end."

Aubrey nodded, but asked him, "Can I just give you a cashier's check for the whole amount now?"

He'd actually never had a client ask that, so he nodded, and said, "Sure, if you think you'll be happy."

Their food arrived, and they ate.

This morning there was very little conversation while they ate their food, unlike the night before. It wasn't stilted or uncomfortable, just an easy kind of quiet.

When their plates were cleared away, Aubrey reached into her purse, and pulled out a pen, and a cashier's check.

The shock on Cole's face was apparent.

She signed her copy of the contract, then swapped copies with him so he could sign hers while she signed his. After that was done, she gave him his copy back, along with the cashier's check.

Cole looked down at the check, and was confused. It was a good five thousand over his bid. "This isn't the right amount," He said to Aubrey.

She leaned forward, and took his hand now. "You see, I may have no experience in these matters, but as I said, my mother does." She squeezed his hand with hers. "She told me what this would cost and also told me you'd give me a break since you're friends with her and my father. I don't want either of us to feel cheated so that little extra, well, that's to ensure I get my money's worth."

She couldn't have surprised him more. "Well, I better get started then," He replied.

"You better," Aubrey said as she slid out of the booth.

# Chapter 8

They arrived back at the house, and Cole followed Aubrey inside. As she placed her purse on the table, her sandal caught the tip of the floorboard that came up the night before, almost tripping her. She looked at Cole, and said, "I wanted to ask you about that," and pointed down to the loosened board. Her sandal actually lifted it up this time.

Cole smiled and crouched down to set the floor board back in place, when he stopped. Looking up at Aubrey, he asked her, "Do you have a flashlight by chance?"

When she shook her head no, he nodded and went out to his truck to grab one. After coming back in, he had the flashlight, along with a hammer. Using the flat end of the hammer, he jimmied the board loose so it came up completely.

"What is it?" Aubrey asked him, concerned. She would be pissed if there were termites in the house.

Turning on the flashlight, Cole reached down into the void beneath the floor board, and pulled out a bag with an envelope inside of it.

Aubrey took the bag from him, and walked into the kitchen while Cole replaced the floor board, nailing it in place so it wouldn't come up again.

By the time he got into the kitchen, Aubrey was standing at the counter, with the bag opened. She was laying out what looked like letters, along with some old pictures.

Cole picked up one of the pictures and looked at it while Aubrey started to read one of the letters out loud.....

*My Love,*

*I know that this is a difficult time for us, being separated by our circumstances. I promise that this is temporary, and long for the time that we will be together, unimpeded by this agonizing situation.*

*All My Love,*

*W*

Aubrey set the letter down, and stared at Cole.

"These pictures," He said, as he handed them over to her, "They're definitely old."

Looking down at the images, Aubrey wanted to cry for some reason. There was one with a young woman, a very proper looking man, and a little girl in it. All of them were smiling.

In another one, there was just the little girl, swinging on a swing. Looking closer at the picture, Aubrey's brow furrowed. "Cole," She said, "I think this was taken in the back yard."

Without waiting for him to follow, Aubrey walked through the breakfast nook, and out the back door. She went down the steps of the back porch, and kept walking until she was about halfway through the yard.

Cole stood on the back stoop and watched her as she would look at the picture, then adjust where she stood. She finally stopped a few minutes later, and motioned for him to join her.

"See," Aubrey said, and held up the picture.

He could see what she was saying, although when the picture was taken, there wasn't a back porch on the house. "Who do you think this is?" He asked her.

Looking down at the picture, the little girl's smile pulling her into the moment, Aubrey smiled, and answered, "I don't know, but I'm going to find out."

They walked back into the house, to look over the letters and see if they could find a clue.


An hour later, Cole asked Aubrey, "Are you going to stare at those pictures and read those letters all day, or are we going to decide when you want my crew to start working on your house?"

Pulling herself out of her mind fog, Aubrey looked up at him, and smiled. "I'm sorry," She said sincerely. "I just get so wrapped up in things mentally, and forget to stop and actually live."

Cole nodded and caressed her cheek with his palm. "Are you like this when you write?" He asked.

"Worse, if you can believe it," Aubrey answered. "My editor and agent take turns making sure I've slept and eaten when I'm working on a book."

He wouldn't lie, that seemed odd, and he told her so, "That's worrisome."

Waving it off, Aubrey replied, "It's not as bad as all that, I'm being dramatic."

The way she played it off though, made Cole wonder if she really was being "dramatic." He would ask her father about it when they met up for dinner that evening. "So, are we still on for tonight?" He asked, "And, when can my guys start coming over and invading your house?"

Taking a deep breath, to try and focus on the conversation, and not the letters and pictures she discovered hidden in her floor board, Aubrey smiled. "Yes, we're on for dinner, I'll call Mom in a few minutes and let her know you're joining us, and the guys can start ASAP."

Feeling a little better about leaving her, Cole leaned over and kissed her on the cheek. "Okay, I'll take off then, we're finishing up another place today so we'll be here first thing, tomorrow morning, okay?"

Aubrey nodded, "Sounds great!" She said, getting excited.

She walked Cole to the front door, and gave him a quick kiss. "Not too much, you work for me starting tomorrow."

"Yes, ma'am," He answered sweetly, and walked out to his truck.

When Aubrey went back inside the house, she automatically went to the kitchen and picked up the letters once again. Walking over to the window seat, she sat down, the morning sun shining in and illuminating the paper. The words pulled her in.


*My Love,*

*I know how this troubles you. Do not worry about me, I'm much stronger than I look. We will get through this together. It will take time, but I have faith that we will make it. I ache to have you hold me, as you did that first night. My dreams are filled with your face, your touch, and knowing you love me makes my days feel happy. My heart is free and flies when I think about our future.*

*All My Love,*

*M*

"So," Aubrey said, "We've got an M and a W?" She pulled out the pictures, studying them again, "Who are you?" She asked to no one. For a quick moment, Aubrey thought she heard the woman's crying, like she did the night before. A cold chill ran up her spine, and she finally put the letters and pictures back in the envelope.

Her phone rang then, looking at it, Aubrey smiled, and hit the button. "Mom," She said brightly, "I hope it's okay if I invite Cole to have dinner with us tonight?"

Christine smiled, "That's fine, honey."

"Did you need me to bring anything?" Aubrey asked her mother.

Pulling out of the driveway, onto Hwy W, Christine switched her phone over to the car's Bluetooth, and answered, "No, honey, we have it all fixed, you and Cole just come and have a good time."

Suddenly feeling silly, Aubrey asked, "Mom," she shook her head at her own silliness, "Can you text me your address please?"

Smiling at her daughter's embarrassment, Christine told her, "Don't worry, Cole knows where it is." She loved her daughter, but knew Aubrey had an artist's mind. And that meant, if she was writing or into something, then all other rational thought seemed to leave her head. "You just go to work, and we'll be fine."

"Bye," Aubrey said, and hung up the phone. She really was lucky that her parents understood her idiosyncrasies.

Just then, her agent called, and Aubrey's mind was now taken up with her actual job. "Sharon," She said into the phone, smiling.

Sharon Riley had been A.J. Sloan's agent for a decade, and still loved the woman to bits, even if she was flaky sometimes. "Well," She said with mock sternness, "I left you alone for five days so you could move out to the backwoods, are you ready to work now?"

Aubrey laughed, "Yes, Sharon, I am." She grabbed a pen and paper, "What's up?"


They stayed on the phone for an hour, with what Aubrey liked to refer to as chaotic negotiations. Sharon desperately wanted her to do a book tour for the new series, and Aubrey hated doing them. Finally, she agreed to do something semi-locally in Milwaukee, Chicago, and Minneapolis. It was the best compromise Aubrey could figure out at the moment. She knew eventually she'd have to go back out to California, but right now, she wanted to stay put.

Walking into the living room, Aubrey realized that she would need to move her blow up mattress, and her bags to make room for Cole's crew to come in and do their jobs.

She called Roesing Furniture, and asked for Jess.

Her friend came on the line and greeted her, "Hello, this is Jess, how can I help you?"

The woman sure did know her customer service, Aubrey thought to herself. "Hello, this is your crazy writer friend, and I need some furniture."

Jess laughed, "I'm sure we can hook you up, what do you need?" She asked Aubrey.

They talked about a full-sized bed, a small dresser, and a desk, and Jess promised to have it delivered later that day.

Aubrey went downstairs into the basement. There was quite a bit of natural light coming in the high windows, so it wasn't as scary as she first thought. It didn't smell like a damp basement, so that was a plus.

After poking into the built in cabinets, Aubrey actually realized there was quite a bit of storage here. She could put a lot of her research stuff here when it came in. It was all still in California, under Sharon's watchful eye.

Going into the adjoining bedroom, Aubrey looked around, it wasn't bad, a little oddly shaped, but it would do, for now.

Taking out her trusty notepad, she thought of Cole, and him taking notes on the house. Was that only yesterday? It felt like she'd known him for ages. The intensity of her thoughts for him scared her a little.  Not that she'd never been in a relationship......she'd just never wanted to jump a man's bones after knowing him less than twenty-four hours.

Smiling to herself, she finished her list of things she needed, and headed out of the bedroom to go upstairs.

She was about halfway through the family room, when she heard the sound of a woman crying again.  This time, it was louder, and not just some figment of her imagination.  Aubrey knew she'd heard it.

The hair on the back of her neck stood up, and Aubrey waited a minute.  The sound seemed to fade, but she thought it sounded as if it was coming from that fruit cellar room.  "Well, I'm too much of a chicken to investigate," She said aloud to the room, "I'm just going to go now, and I'll see you later."  And she practically ran up the stairs, grabbed her keys and purse, and went down to the store.


Picking out a light beige color for the walls of the bedroom, Aubrey found herself in the bedding area for the second time.  This time, she wasn't really seeing the options of bedding, she was wondering why she was hearing a woman crying in her house.

Was that the woman in the pictures?  Was it the little girl?

Either way, it made Aubrey uneasy. So she'd bought a
house with a little mystery attached to it? It shouldn't
bother her since her job basically revolved around mystery
and suspense, but there was just a little niggling of fear
when she thought about it.

Finally, she snapped out of her mind fog, and picked
up a beautiful bed set with red, black, and a beige that
would match the walls.

She checked out, and got into the car and started to
drive home, when she realized she had no groceries.

"Crap!" She said aloud, and pulled into the grocery
store parking lot.

Another hour was spent figuring out what to stock her
kitchen with. The next four to six weeks would be spent
eating off of paper plates.

Excitement for her mom's cooking was the only thing
keeping Aubrey from sinking into a well of doubts. Had
she bit off more than she could chew? Perhaps, but it was
her money and her life, so if she screwed up, at least she
did it on her own terms.

Leaving the grocery store, Aubrey drove home. As
soon as she got through the back door, she listened to see if
her weeping lady was still at it. There were no sounds in
the house, and relief washed over her.

"Thanks," She shouted out, and went to put the bags of groceries in the kitchen.

By the time she was finished with putting things away, Aubrey estimated that she would have just enough time to paint the downstairs bedroom before the furniture arrived.

Her painting materials in hand, she set everything up and got to work.

Luckily, painting a room was something she actually had some experience in. She'd gone to a few painting parties when friends bought houses in California, and had the basics down.

It only took her an hour and a half to finish painting the room, which wasn't bad for a relative amateur. Her music was blaring, a mix of hip hop, and rock.....to keep her in the work zone.

She hadn't heard Cole come in and practically jumped out of her skin when she turned around, and saw him standing in the doorway.


Cole had knocked and knew Aubrey was home when he saw her car in the driveway. He walked around to the back door, and heard the music, so he went in. "Hey, I called out, when I came in," He said to her, trying to explain.

Smiling, Aubrey responded, "I'm sure you did, I had the music blaring. Sorry." She walked over and gave him a quick kiss before asking him, "What are you doing here?"

She was so cute, with paint splattered over her cheeks. She wore cutoff shorts that nicely framed her backside, along with a tank top that read UCLA on it. The fact that she looked years younger than she was only made him more affected by her beauty. "Uh," He tried to remember why he was here, "I wanted to drop off some stuff to prep for tomorrow," he almost mumbled the words.

Aubrey wasn't so blind, she didn't recognize male appreciation when she saw it. Just to tease him, she made sure she walked with a little more hip action as she went over to turn down her music. "Well," She turned around to tease him, "why don't you put your things upstairs and then we'll see what we can do for lunch."

Cole wasn't about to turn down that invitation, especially when she talked like that. He nodded, and turned to go back upstairs. As he walked through the family room, he felt a blast of cold air. It was so cold, that it actually stopped Cole in his tracks. As quickly as he felt the cold, it went away. Thinking maybe he had better check out the furnace when they did the renovations, Cole went upstairs.

# Chapter 9

Aubrey cleaned up her mess and went upstairs.

Cole was making trips in and out of the front door, while she made them up some sandwiches for lunch. Her day had been relatively productive so far.

When he finally joined her in the kitchen, Aubrey slid a plate over to him and smiled, "It's the best you'll get right now."

Taking a bite, Cole didn't mind one bit. Most of his work days were spent consuming lunch on the fly, so he wasn't too discerning when it came to food. "So, what made you paint the room downstairs?" He asked Aubrey in between bites.

Shrugging, Aubrey replied, "Well, I realized that tomorrow you and your guys will be knee deep upstairs, and I needed somewhere to work that was a little more private." She took a sip of her bottle water, and added, "And I called my friend Jess, over at Roesing Furniture, they're delivering a few pieces for me today so I'm off the air mattress." She gave him a thumbs up.

Nodding to her, Cole commented, "Well, that's good." He looked around, and asked her, "Are you ready for the onslaught of crazy that is about to descend upon you tomorrow?"

Aubrey thought a lot about it, how the house would look when she was done with the renovations. It would be a home for her, and that was why she moved here. "Yes," She said, then told him, "Although I'm about to start a new book series so I'm slightly nervous about juggling it all."

Shaking his head, Cole offered, "That's what you have me for, I'll try not to bother you unless it's necessary." He smiled, "But I've never done this kind of renovation with the owner still occupying the house, so it will be a new experience for both of us."

Wondering if she should tell Cole about her "crying woman," Aubrey just stood there, and ate her sandwich. She was about to say something when there was a knock on the front door. "That must be the furniture delivery guys," She said, and went to answer it.

Sure enough, it was a big truck from Roesing's. The two delivery men smiled and asked where she wanted the furniture placed. She showed them downstairs. Cole was already down there, making sure everything was cleared from the room, and checking the paint to ensure it had dried. She couldn't help but smile at the sweetness of his gesture.

Within minutes, there was a bed, a dresser, and a desk neatly placed in the room.

Aubrey tipped the guys, they each gave her a big smile, so she must've given them a good one. Then she went back downstairs, and found Cole pulling the bedding out of the bags from the store.

"What are you doing?" Aubrey asked him, her hands on her hips.

Smiling, Cole answered, "I'm pulling out the bedding for the bed. "Do you want to wash it first?" He asked her.

Aubrey laughed, "I know I should, but I just want to make the bed," she told him.

"Okay," He said, and they made up the bed together.

There was something really intimate about making up a bed with a man and Aubrey felt the zing of arousal. Once the last pillow had a case on it, she plopped down on the bed, and patted a spot beside her for Cole.

He sat down next to her, on her bed, and wanted nothing more than to peel off her clothes and make love with her. Cole would never make love TO a woman like Aubrey, it would be a shared experience, he was sure of it.

Aubrey could see the look in his eyes, and knew his thoughts matched hers. "We definitely have time," She started to say, "but I'm a little worried about taking this further."

There was that mind and mouth he admired. "Can I ask why?"

"Partly because of the renovations, I'm afraid of a conflict," She explained, "and partly because I don't want to just fool around in my guest bedroom, I want to be in my new master suite, surrounded by candles, and my huge king-sized bed, and use every inch of it to explore one another."

Her words, so descriptive, made him hard. "Well," He said, and cleared his throat, "You'll definitely have me on the edge of my seat waiting until then."

Turning to face him, Aubrey looked into his blue eyes, and noticed that they had little specks of gray in them. "I promise," She told him, "that I want to be much more than friends with you Cole, I just want to keep my life organized right now."

Cole cupped her face and smiled, before saying, "I think you're going to learn, Aubrey, that there is nothing organized about what's going on between us." He released her face, and slapped his palms onto his thighs before standing up. "Well, I do have a job, so I'll go do that, and I'll pick you up about five-thirty if that's okay, so we can go out to your parents' place."

Knowing he was right, in what he was saying, but thinking she could control things a little longer, Aubrey smiled, and stood up. "That sounds good," She replied, and stayed where she was after he nodded, and left.

After she heard the door close upstairs, she plopped back down on the bed and wondered what she was going to do about Cole Rafferty and the monkey wrench he was throwing into her plans.

Aubrey spent the remainder of the afternoon setting up her computer on her new desk. Since she was anything but tech savvy, she made sure to get something that she only had to plug in. The cable guy came by to hook up her internet, so she was now "accessible." The thought brought her both happiness and apprehension. The happiness was for checking her social media and keeping in touch with friends, the apprehension was because now Sharon could reach her, along with the other members of her team.

The success she'd achieved was great and she wouldn't trade it for anything. After all, it's what bought this house and made her life a lot easier. She actually had a retirement account, and would be comfortable for the rest of her life. She wasn't in the realm of the greats, but she was proud of her work. And if all she had to do was write, then her life would be blissful. She didn't anticipate the trappings that came with being successful and those were the things she dreaded.

She sat at her computer, and reviewed some notes for her newest book. After all the background was done, writing it wasn't actually too bad. Aubrey was a detail-oriented person. That meant days of research and plotting. She knew friends who just sat down and wrote, but she had to really think things through before putting them down on the page.

Her mind switched gears and thought about the love letters, sitting upstairs on her kitchen counter. A real life mystery compared to the ones she made up in her mind was simply fascinating.

The pictures intrigued her, but the letters......the letters touched her. Clearly there was a secret romance there. Why would someone need to keep it a secret?

Glancing at the clock on her computer screen, Aubrey yelped. She needed to get ready or they would be late for dinner at her parents' house. She sent Cole a quick text, Please come in the back door, I'm downstairs. Then she grabbed some clothes and ran into the bathroom.


Cole was just getting home when he received Aubrey's text. He knew, logically, that she was just telling him which door to use when he came to pick her up, but he felt like a rubber band pulled a little tauter. He thought about the woman almost all the time now, and it was driving him nuts.

He'd just stepped out of the shower, when his phone rang. "Hello," He answered.

"Oh, there you are," Linda said sweetly. "I'm just calling to confirm what time for our date tomorrow night."

Cole sighed. If he hadn't already promised her, he would've cancelled. "How about 6:30?" He asked.

"Sounds good, I'll see you then," Linda purred into the phone.

After he hung up, Cole shook his head. He would need to make sure that Linda understood they were just friends. If he wasn't sure before, after meeting Aubrey, he was damn well sure now.

He started getting ready, putting all thoughts of Linda out of his mind.

Leaving his house, he calculated it would take fifteen minutes to get to Aubrey's place, and then another fifteen to her parents' house. He hated being late, it was his form of OCD he supposed.

Glancing over, he smiled at the flowers he'd picked up on his way home. They were for Mrs. Slojankonkowski. His mom always told him to bring something for the hostess, no matter what.

Aubrey was curling her hair when she heard a noise upstairs. She listened, and smiled when she heard Cole shout, "It's me, Cole," down the stairs.

"Come on down," She shouted back. He was being sweet, and she appreciated that. There weren't a lot of men who understood the importance of that particular character trait. She smiled when she saw his head poke into the doorway leading to the bathroom, and blushed, "Sorry, I'm almost done, I promise," she told him.

Feeling a little bit like a voyeur, he stepped away from the bathroom doorway, and answered, "It's okay, I'm a few minutes early."

He sat down at Aubrey's computer, watching the slide show on her screen saver. There were pictures of beaches, forests, and even some rivers. They were spectacular pictures. When he heard Aubrey behind him he turned, smiled, and asked her, "Did you take these?"

Aubrey's eyes widened, "Me?" She asked, then answered "No." She smiled as she looked at the landscapes, "A friend of mine works for National Geographic and gets to go to the far ends of the earth." She smiled down at Cole and placed her hands on his shoulders. "I could never be that artistic."

Spinning the chair around so he was facing Aubrey, he asked her, "Why are you so self-deprecating?"

Without missing a beat, she answered, "I'm a neurotic writer who struggles with self-esteem issues, and I'm a girl." She shrugged, "That should pretty much explain that."

Cole laughed, and said, "I guess so then." He stood, and really looked at her now, her dark curled tresses. "You are beautiful," He whispered, then leaned down to kiss her.

The kiss was a sweet one, but Aubrey felt as though it was just a preview, and looked forward to the main feature, later on.

"Should we go?" He asked her, glancing at his watch.

Nodding, Aubrey picked up her bag, and commented, "I'm glad to know I'm not the only one with a few neuroses."

Even though he didn't comment, Cole just smiled, and followed her upstairs. He waited for Aubrey to grab a bottle of wine out of the refrigerator, then held the door for her. She diligently locked it behind her, which made him feel better, and they headed around the house to where his car was parked.

When he opened the car door, and made sure she was in and buckled before he went around to get in the driver's seat, Aubrey felt safe.

"Are you always so attentive?" She asked him as he started up the car.

Looking both ways, before pulling out onto Duane Street, Cole waited until he was on the road before answering, "My mother was very insistent about my manners where the girls were concerned."

"Oh, a manners Nazi," Aubrey said jokingly.

Cole's face fell, "Actually," he explained, "she was abused by her first husband, and was sure as hell not going to have her son turn out that way."

The slap of the words hit Aubrey quickly. "Oh, Cole, I'm sorry, I didn't mean to be such a jerk."

Moving his hand, so it covered hers on the counsel between them, Cole smiled, "It's okay, Aubrey, you didn't know."

Suddenly feeling stupid, Aubrey was silent. She couldn't believe she'd been so callous. He was right, she didn't know, but still, she should learn to watch what she said.

Sensing that she was embarrassed, Cole tried to sound upbeat, "Listen, it was an honest mistake, let's not let it ruin our evening."

Aubrey appreciated his consideration. "I'll try, but I make no guarantees." She began, "I hate feeling stupid and right now, I feel awful."

A few minutes later, Cole turned onto Hwy 11 East. They passed the Haylofter's theater, where Aubrey did her first "official" acting role. After turning onto Hwy W, they passed the large cemetery, and Aubrey said a prayer as she passed it. A couple of her friends form high school were buried there.

Just before they came to Hwy A, they made a right turn onto a long driveway.  Aubrey was curious because she didn't remember there being a house out here.

They seemed to drive for a while before a tree line came into sight, and you could clearly see a house set behind it. "Wow!" Aubrey whispered.

Cole pulled the sedan up next to the house, "If you think that's cool, wait until you see the inside," he told her.

## Chapter 10

Aubrey's parents came out onto the front porch to greet them. "Hey there," Christine said to them.

Cole helped Aubrey out, then opened the back door to get the flowers out. As they reached the porch, Aubrey handed her father the bottle of wine and Cole gave her mother the flowers.

Greg and Christine looked at one another, wide smiles on their faces.

The foursome went inside and Aubrey almost gasped at what she saw. Her parents' house was like one in a magazine! She stared at her mother, who then pointed to Cole, "He did it!"

They all laughed.

"I can't believe it," Aubrey said as she and her mother went into the large kitchen to place the flowers in a vase. The men went out the back doors to the barbeque grill.

Christine smiled, "I know, sometimes I pinch myself." She said to her daughter. After placing the flowers in the long table in the dining room, she sat down. "It was an absolute mess when we found it," She explained to Aubrey, "Dad called Cole and asked him to come over and look at it before we made an offer." Looking out, Christine watched her husband making grand gestures over the grill. He was such a character! She turned back to her daughter, "So, we went through every inch of it with Cole." She smiled, "I told him what I wanted, and he told me what he could do, and we just bought it."

Standing up, Aubrey walked through the rooms. For some reason, her mother didn't accompany her, but Aubrey didn't mind. She started with the great room, just off the kitchen. The room spanned the entire length of the first floor. It was painted white, but had one wall that was white and blue striped. The blue stripes were used in accents as well. It was so pristine, Aubrey felt weird sitting down on the furniture.

"What do you think?" Christine came in, and asked her daughter.

Turning around, Aubrey shook her head and sighed, before answering, "It's gorgeous."

Christine absently ran her hand over the back of the sofa, "It was an old farmhouse, with all these little rooms, but Cole just opened it all up."

Aubrey could see that there was some preservation in the renovations as well. A door here, a wall accent there, the combination of it all just came out as tasteful.

Hearing the guys come in the back door, Christine motioned for Aubrey to join her, and they walked back into the kitchen.

The men brought in a large platter with chicken and steak on it.

Christine made a tossed salad and baked potatoes to complete the dinner, and the foursome sat down at the table.

Aubrey turned to Cole, and said, "You did a great job on the renovations."

Cole laughed, and pointed to her mom, before answering, "It's a little easier when you're shown pictures out of magazines and told to make it happen."

Blushing, Christine nodded, and said, "Yep, that's about how it happened." She pointed back at Cole, "But not everyone can do what you did."

Making a slight bow, Cole returned, "You are right about that," in an exaggerated voice, making everyone laugh.

During dinner, the conversation gravitated around, what else but the renovations that Aubrey had in mind for her home. By the time they'd gone over it, both her parents were looking at her like she'd lost her mind.

"What?" She asked out loud.

Greg looked at his daughter, "We didn't live here while the renovations were going on." He told her.

Aubrey played it off, "I'm in the basement now, and that's basically finished. The guys will do the 2nd floor and main floor, and then I'll move upstairs while they do a touch up on the basement."

Even though her plan was a good one, she still sat there with two sets of parental eyes giving her the "we know what's best for you" looks.

Cole wanted to save Aubrey, so he complimented the food. Once the conversation steered away from her house, Aubrey shot him a look of thanks.

"How did you sleep last night?" Her father asked her when they went out to the back patio for dessert.

Shaking her head, she told him, "Not too well, I guess, I woke up with tears again, but I really don't remember having a tough time sleeping or any bad dreams."

Looking worried again, Greg asked her, "Do you want me to ask a colleague to prescribe you some anti-anxiety medication, I can refer you to a few doctors who would meet with you."

Touching her dad's arm, Aubrey smiled, "Thank you, but no, not right now anyway." She looked over at Cole and her mother talking about the flowers she'd recently planted around the patio. "I'm not feeling really stressed out."

"That doesn't mean you're not stressed out on the inside," Greg informed her.

She wanted to tell her dad about the noises she'd been hearing, but felt like it made her sound crazy. Instead, she reassured him with, "If I have trouble sleeping in a week, I'll call you and ask you to help me make an appointment."

Relieved that she was at least taking his advice, Greg smiled. "Okay," He said, and kissed her on the forehead.

For dessert, her mom made homemade apple pie, and her dad piped up to say that he bought the vanilla ice cream for topping. They dug in and ate until everyone was stuffed. Not long after, Aubrey and Cole said goodnight to her parents. Cole was loaded down with leftovers, and walked out to the car.

"Thank you for coming with me," Aubrey told him as they were driving back down the driveway.

Smiling, Cole answered, "It was my pleasure."

Reaching over, Aubrey placed her hand on his arm, and ran her fingers down the full length of it. Her fingertips made his skin sensitive, and he looked over at her. With the sun setting, her eyes sparkled as the golden rays hit them through the window. She looked as if she were something out of a movie. "It's hard to concentrate when you're doing that," He said softly, but turned his eyes back to the road.

"I think that's the point," Aubrey returned.

Her fingertips were only the beginning. Her words practically whispered along his skin making him swallow with great effort. "Aubrey, what happened to just friends?" He asked her, trying to distract her.

Pulling her hand off of his arm, Aubrey replied, "You're right, of course, I apologize."

If her words were warmth, his seemed to be ice cold. He could feel her retreat into herself, and cussed at himself mentally for it. He didn't want to be just friends with this woman, he wanted to be in her bed, and have her in his bed and make love until neither of them could walk or talk.

He waited until he'd pulled into her driveway, before he said anything else. "I was teasing you," He told her, "and it upset you. I'm sorry."

Teasing? Aubrey rolled the word around in her mind. "I'm feeling all torn up right now," She looked at him. "I want.......you, and I want my house, and I want peace, and I want to write." He nodded and she smiled, "But it seems wanting and having all of those things is very tough."

"I can see that," Cole said, his hand on hers.

Sighing, Aubrey brought his hand up to her lips and kissed it, "I think we should be just friends, but I certainly don't want to be just friends, does that make sense?" She asked him.

Cole tugged their joined hands toward his lips, and kissed the back of her hand, before replying, "It makes perfect sense to me."

They both laughed, and tilted their heads together. "No sense in staying in your car and fogging up the windows so the neighbors think we're sleeping together," Aubrey whispered.

Shaking his head, at her ability to find humor in even the most awkward of moments, Cole nodded and got out of the car. They went in the back door of the house, and Aubrey flipped on lights as they went.

"It feels too big and empty right now, so I get a little freaked out and need lights on." Aubrey explained, "After I'm settled, I turn them off, but it's still new." She offered him a bottled water from the refrigerator, which he gladly took, and commented, "Not sure how it will feel being downstairs."

After taking a generous swallow of his water, partly to soothe his insides from being incinerated with the heat they generated together, Cole said, "You know, you can always stay at my place, or I can stay here."

The offer, although generous, and far too tempting for Aubrey's good, was one she couldn't accept. "I'm pretty sure that would totally encourage the talk with the neighbors." She used the words lightly, in an effort to diffuse the sparks between them.

"So what!" Cole snapped back. He hadn't meant to, it's just that he was getting really foggy in the head where Aubrey Slojankonkowski was concerned. Hell, he could even pronounce her name correctly, he'd actually been practicing it. While he worked on her folks' place, he'd always used "Mr. and Mrs. S," when addressing them. Now he found himself learning dictation and making sure he knew all the recent information about her. He knew her last book was #4 on the New York Times Best Seller List. He knew that she liked chocolate ice cream because it was in an interview he pulled up on YouTube.

Watching Cole pace the length of the breakfast nook, Aubrey could see the wheels turning in his mind. Lord knew, she'd done that plenty of times herself. "I know," She said softly, "that we're both a little revved up right now." He stopped, shot her a look, and then continued pacing. "Why don't we just say we'll see each other, and then we'll sleep together after the house is done?"

Her words stopped him dead in his tracks, "How do you make it sound so easy?" He asked her, sarcasm dripping from the words.

Anger, fast and sharp, traveled through her body. Without missing a beat, she stepped forward, grabbed him, and kissed him. Her hands wrapped around his neck as if he were the only thing keeping her from drowning. Her tongue silently pleaded with his lips for entrance, and she sighed when he granted it. The only sound in the room was their breaths as they mingled.

Cole felt as if he'd suffered whiplash, his feelings turned from anger to lust in the space of a heartbeat. She felt perfect in his arms, her body fit against his as if it were meant to be there. As if the Lord had made each of them this way so they fit together just like this. He kissed her, and indulged on her mouth as if it contained the last drop of water on earth. And he couldn't get enough.

Running her hands through Cole's hair, Aubrey hummed with energy. Each touch and each taste just amplified how they both felt.......alive.

Aubrey was the first to pull away, trying to gasp for breath. "Well, that's one way to shut you up I guess," She whispered, trying to joke.

Cole pushed her hair back with his hands, loving how soft it felt between his fingers. Her hair was a dark brown, almost black depending on the lighting and looked the color of rosewood. Her eyes were blue as the sky normally, but now, now they were infused with a dark blue, like the deep ocean, and he knew they could swallow him up if he allowed them to. "What is it?" He asked her, "This connection between us?"

Still trying to catch her breath, Aubrey answered, "I honestly don't know, but it feels so good."

Growling, Cole took a step away from her. "When you say things like that it's like adding gasoline to an already huge fire."

"I know," Aubrey said to him, her face serious, "That's why I do it, I want to see how hot it will get."

Using the small reserve of willpower he still had, Cole managed to keep from grabbing her and kissing her again, saying, "Well, if you keep talking like that, it will get a lot hotter."

Aubrey smiled, not to mock him, but because kissing him was liberating. It was setting her heart free to roam the whole wide world, and she'd never had that before. "I'll just bet it would, Cole Rafferty."

## Chapter 11

A few hours later, Aubrey was sitting downstairs, in her new "room" and staring at the computer screen before her.

Cole left......reluctantly.....a few hours earlier. They'd reached some sort of agreement, although Aubrey wasn't sure exactly what it was. When she was around him, she wanted everything. It was this all-consuming need that she couldn't quench, couldn't sate, and couldn't satisfy. After he left, she came down here, half dazed from his kisses, and tried to work on her new book.

Now, she found herself in a situation she'd never been before. She didn't feel like writing.

Instead, she went back upstairs, grabbed another bottle of water, and grabbed the bag with the letters and pictures in it.

After returning to her basement room, she spread out the letters and pictures over the top of her brand new dresser. Standing back, she tried to get a mental impression of the situation.

M:

*The fact that you are willing to truly listen to my ideas is thrilling. I'm so used to being cast aside as if I were a nuisance, then brought out (like the good china and silver) to impress when needed. How freeing it is to feel as though someone values me for being just who I am. Your thoughts, are so closely connected to mine, that I feel we are one. Please do not lose faith, we will make this work.*

*All My Love,*

*W*

Aubrey read the letter, and an idea dawned on her. This letter was a description of what was happening between her and Cole, almost verbatim.

She sat down at her desk and re-read the letters. There were ten of them in all and, with no dates, it was difficult to figure out which ones came first. They were careful, Aubrey had to admit it, as if they knew someone could happen upon the letters and read them. Sure the reader would know there was a romance, but would be hard pressed to accuse.

Suddenly, Aubrey felt really tired. The craziness of the last couple of days had caught up to her and she needed some sleep.

After washing up, she grabbed an oversized t-shirt, and braided her long hair, before crawling into the bed. Having an actual bed, that felt wonderful, she was lulled to sleep immediately.

*She was walking outside, into the sunshine and it was beautiful. There was a little girl playing in the yard, but Aubrey didn't know who she was. She was saying something to Aubrey, calling out to her but Aubrey wasn't able to answer. She reached out her hand to the little girl....*

Waking up with a start, Aubrey sat straight up in bed. She was covered in sweat, and exhausted. Swiping at her cheeks, she felt the wetness of shed tears on them and wondered what in the hell was going on. Looking over at the clock, she saw it was only seven in the morning. Cole's crew wouldn't be here until eight so she had some time yet.

With a smile, she quickly shrugged off the remaining fragments of sleep, formed a plan, and jumped out of bed.

At 7:55am, Cole's crews pulled up and parked in front of Aubrey's house. He hadn't slept well, all the want inside of him keeping him from seeking the refuge of sleep. At least he would see her, every day, for the next four to six weeks. It may very well be torture, but he had a sneaking suspicion it would be an exquisite torture.

They were getting out of the trucks when Aubrey came out the front door. She was smiling, and gave a bright, "Good morning guys, come on in and have some coffee and donuts."

His guys didn't need to be told twice, and headed in.
At least they all said hi to her, which was a good sign. He
was the last one in and was, somehow, able to refrain from
kissing her.


Handing out coffee and donuts was fun for Aubrey.
She wanted the guys to feel okay around her. They would
be here for the next month and then some and she didn't
want to feel like they were strangers. "Okay, who's who?"
She asked the group.

Cole should have guessed she would want to know
who was working here. He made the introductions, "This
is Zeke, my supervisor, and then we have Mark, Oliver,
Trace, Woody, and our young apprentice, Max."

Aubrey nodded and took note of the men. Zeke was
huge, like a giant bear, so she'd never forget him. Mark
and Oliver were lanky and tall so she might get them mixed
up a little, Trace was the pretty boy of this group, if one
excluded Cole, Woody was, well, like a piece of wood, light
hair, light skin, and an almost square face, and lastly, Max.
Max was a baby compared to the rest. "I'm Aubrey, so
please call me Aubrey." She looked at all of the men,
making sure to make eye contact. "I know I'll try to stay
out of your way and keep to my rooms downstairs."

All the men smiled, some making gestures of
acknowledgement. Cole just smiled. They were all half in

love with her now; Heaven help them. "Okay," Cole clapped his hands together to turn the men's attentions to him, "we've gone over the plan so let's get to work." He looked at Aubrey, "It's the master suite first."

Knowing that was the room with the most work to be done, Aubrey felt it made sense. Not that she had much of a say as now it was Cole's area of expertise. "I'll be downstairs if you need me," She said to him, and smiled to the guys as she left. She could hear the murmurs of "sweet lady," and "good coffee," as she walked downstairs and figured she'd done well.


Hours later, Aubrey was at her computer, and actually writing her new book, when she heard a knock on the doorway. She intentionally left the door open so the men, specifically Cole, knew she was available to speak to them.

"Hi," Cole said from the doorway of the basement bedroom. He'd been watching her for a good five minutes. She was fascinating to watch as she wrote. Her facial expressions were clearly revealing what her character was doing; something good, something funny, or something bad. He'd never seen someone write before, so the experience was a new one for him.

Since Cole wasn't saying anything, Aubrey asked him, "Is there something you needed?"

Her question brought him out of his thoughts. "Oh,"
He looked embarrassed, "Yes, um, we've run into a snag."

That didn't sound good to Aubrey. She nodded, and
got up to follow him upstairs.

"I told the guys to go ahead and get lunch, and that
way we could discuss your options." Cole told her as they
climbed the stairs up to the second floor.

She smiled, confident that he could fix anything,
"Sure."

They walked into the master bedroom, and Aubrey's
face was slack with shock. The room wasn't a room
anymore. It was a shell. They'd completely removed the
lathe and plaster on the walls so she could see where the
electrical was run. "So," She looked at Cole, and asked,
"What's the snag?"

Before he could answer, Cole heard a shout of, "Is
anyone home?" coming from downstairs. He smiled, and
asked Aubrey to "stay there for a moment." He came back
into the room a few minutes later. "Aubrey
Slojankonkowski, please meet a colleague of mine, and
architect, Sean McAdams."

Aubrey reached out and shook Sean's hand. "Hi," She
said in greeting and waited for them to explain.

Cole started in, and said, "Okay, Sean, I was just about
to explain to Aubrey about our issue."

Sean nodded and looked at Aubrey, "It appears that when they took down the wall that separated these two rooms to make them into one big room, they didn't do it the right way."

Aubrey looked above them, and saw some strategically placed holes. "Oh?" She asked him.

Cole stood next to her while Sean poked around with a flashlight for a few minutes. When he re-joined them, he said, "Not a problem, we can reconfigure some joists in the attic and then I'd say you re-wire while you're at it."

Aubrey looked between the men, a little lost, and wondering what they needed her for.

Finally, Cole turned to Aubrey, and told her, "For you, the owner, it means a little more money, and about 2 – 3 days delay if we can't find an electrician right away."

Shrugging, Aubrey said, "Okay, you've got this, I'm going back down to write," and turned to leave the room. Both men just stared after her, shocked by her disinterest.

She was in the kitchen a few minutes later, making up a ham sandwich when Sean came in. The smile he wore was a wicked one, in Aubrey's mind. She smiled back, and asked him, "What can I help you with?"

Leaning against the counter, Sean crossed his arms and said, "So, you're the big time writer who has come home to hang around the rabble."

"No one I know uses the word rabble anymore," She returned, "And yes, I guess I am the big-time writer."

He reached into his briefcase and pulled out a copy of one of her books, asking, "Would you mind signing it?"

Laughing, because the conversation was so odd, and yet amusing at the same time, Aubrey gladly took the book from him and signed it with a flourish. "There you go," She said when she'd finished, and handed it back.

"This place will be fantastic when you're done with it, if Cole has any say," Sean told her.

Aubrey realized two things about Sean McAdams in the few minutes she'd known him. The first was that he respected Cole's work, and the second was that he was gay. Of course, he did a pretty good job of hiding it, but she had enough openly gay friends to recognize someone not keen on publicizing. "I think, Sean, that we are about to become very good friends," She told him.

Leaning back against the counter, Sean replied, "I think you're absolutely right."


When Aubrey finally got back to work, after talking with Sean for a good half hour about a variety of things, she allowed herself to be lost in her new story.

At some point, Cole came back downstairs and, yet again, knocked softly on the doorframe.

When she pushed away from her desk, a smile was firmly planted on her face. "How's it going?" She asked him.

Nodding, Cole replied, "Good actually, we already have some joists ordered, and they'll be here tomorrow, and I found an electrician that I trust." He came in and stood against the wall, smiling, "He'll be here tomorrow too so the delay will only be for about a day."

It all sounded perfectly fine to Aubrey, so why was he looking at her like he was? She asked him, "Is there something you want to talk about?"

Cole didn't think it was a problem but he had to ask, "When we were upstairs, and telling you this problem would cost more money and time, I was wondering why you didn't seem bothered in the least?"

Ah, now she was getting the picture. Aubrey asked him, "And normally your clients get all crazy like on the HGTV channel, right?"

"Well, yes," He answered quickly, "But you never even flinched."

Leaning back in her office chair, Aubrey asked him, "Would you question me if it had something to do with writing books?"

He didn't understand why she would ask that question, but he did answer her, "No."

"Because it's my job, right?" Aubrey asked him.

Cole nodded, "Yes, you're more of an expert on it all than I am." He replied.

Aubrey smiled, "And you are more of an expert on renovations so what do I care if it takes a few more days, I'm perfectly fine down here, and the money, we've already discussed that, and I think you know I'm good for it."

Her words made him laugh. "I understand now."

Sighing, Aubrey said to him, "Cole, I'm a pretty simple woman, not that those two words really go together, but, I digress, I only get passionate about a few things." She stood up and walked over to him, "I'll let you know if I'm going to get pissed about something."

Without waiting for a response, Aubrey leaned in and kissed him. It was a soft brushing of lips, not meant to tease, but it pretty much was just that.

"I'm a mess," Cole told her, and didn't let her lean in to kiss him again. He didn't want to get her dirty. Although, he knew his actions weren't meant to make her feel rejected, he saw a flash of it cross her face before she masked it with a smile. Not wanting to prolong his own physical agony, he smiled and said, "I'll see you," and turned to leave.

Aubrey stood in the room, wondering why he just left like that. When she glanced over at her computer, she was drawn back into her story, and let the thoughts of Cole leave, at least for a while.


When she came up for air, metaphorically speaking, Aubrey's stomach was growling, and the sun was setting. It was Friday night and that meant only one thing......... Fish Fry!

Aubrey was out the door in record time, and in the car. She drove downtown and parked in front of the library. Although it wasn't her destination this evening, she made a mental note to stop in there this week.

Her eyes were focused on, arguably, the best place to get Fish Fry in Burlington, Gabby's Palace.

# Chapter 12

As she crossed the street, she realized how lucky she'd been to even get a parking spot within a two block radius of the place. When she opened the door, the smell of it all hit her full force and it was like heaven. Only a mid-westerner seemed to understand the almost religious experience of Friday Night Fish Fry. It's what she grew up doing with her parents and no one in California had ever understood it.

Gabby's was a family owned business right downtown and, even though the space wasn't huge, the crowds came and ate. Dave, the owner, was a funny guy with a big personality and a laugh to match it.

Aubrey went into the bar entrance. She smiled at the people already playing pool and nursing a beer or cocktail after a hard week at work.

Weaving her way over to the take out counter, she ordered the baked cod, french fries, and cole slaw. The server told her it would be a few minutes before her order was ready so she was more than welcome to sit at the bar and wait.

Smiling at the suggestion, Aubrey made her way to the bar. There were a few people here she thought she went to school with, but she wasn't daring enough to start up a conversation. Luckily, there was an empty seat so she grabbed it. A few minutes later, the bartender made her way over and asked, "What can I getcha?"

"Amaretto Stone Sour, blended," Aubrey replied, and was smiling because that's all she seemed to order when she was in Wisconsin.

With a nod, the bartender left, and went over to make up the drink.

Aubrey used the time to people watch. In such a close proximity, it was easy to hear what others were saying, and getting a feel for the atmosphere was something she thought was crucial for her writing ideas.

There was a couple discussing their kids, and another who were clearly just out for a good time, and another, across the bar........ Recognition dawned on her and all the blood rushed from her head to her feet. It was Cole, and he was here with that woman, what was her name? Oh, yeah, Linda, from the other night.

Jealousy, fresh and sharp, sliced through Aubrey's chest. It wasn't as if she and Cole were exclusive. Heck, it was her suggestion that they stay "just friends" until the work on the house was done, so she couldn't exactly be mad. But here she was, pissed!

The bartender put down her drink, her smile fading as she looked at Aubrey.

Realizing that she was scowling, Aubrey looked over, nodded to the bartender, and threw a bill on the bar, hoping it was enough to cover the drink. Before she made a fool of herself, much like Linda did the other night, Aubrey decided to wait for her food in the dining area. She couldn't help but notice though, before she got up, that Linda slipped her arm around Cole's neck and kissed him as if she were very comfortable doing so and had a lot of practice at it too.

The bartender came back over, saying, "Here's the change for your drink."

Aubrey didn't care, and said, "Just keep it," not realizing she'd given the woman a $50 dollar bill for one drink.

Her food was ready by the time she'd gotten back to the pick-up counter, and Aubrey was relieved. She hadn't even tasted her drink, and gave it to the server saying, "Sorry, don't have time to enjoy this. It's paid for," before leaving.

Aubrey hurriedly crossed the street, jay-walked actually, but her present mind set demanded a quick getaway. "Damn him," She said aloud once she was in the safety of her vehicle.


Inside Gabby's, Linda was smiling. Cole didn't know why, but he suspected she was thinking there was more between them than a casual dinner. He had to extricate himself from her grip on more than one occasion and, by the time they left, he was exhausted. The term, "beating them off with a stick," was stuck firmly in his mind. He was walking down the street to his truck, when he ran into Max, who was also leaving the restaurant. "Hey, Max," Cole said to him.

"Hey," Max returned. "Did you have dinner?" He asked his boss.

Nodding, Cole replied, "Yes, Linda Meyers and I had a dinner date I guess."

Looking at Cole strangely, Max asked, "You guess?" He laughed, "I think she thought it was a whole lot more."

Agreeing with his young employee, Cole said, "Yeah, I know, but it was a onetime deal."

"Well," Max said, his eyebrows raised, "Make sure you tell Miss Aubrey that, she looked really mad when she saw you and that Linda lady together."

All thought left Cole's brain, "Wh, what?" He asked Max.

Nodding back, Max told him, "Yeah she came in, to get food I guess, and I was going to talk to her but she was looking over at you and Linda at the bar, and looked so mad, I steered clear."

Clapping Max on the shoulder, Cole told him, "Thanks for letting me know," and he left quickly.

Aubrey was downstairs, at her desk, sniffling like a fifteen year old, when she heard knocking from upstairs. She made sure to lock the doors when she got home, so she didn't have to answer them.

Her food sat in the take out container, on her dresser, getting cold, but she didn't care. She felt betrayed. There was a knocking on the window of her bedroom, and she jumped. There.....looking down through the glass, was Cole. "Go away!" She yelled at him.

Oh yeah, he thought to himself, she saw him and Linda. "Aubrey, please let me in?" He pleaded. He was down on his knees, spying through a basement window, and he was sure that one of the neighbors would be calling the cops at any moment.

Turning away from him, Aubrey sighed. She had two choices here......1. She could be a baby and refuse, only to have to let him in tomorrow without them resolving this, or 2. She could be an adult and talk to him tonight. The latter was not what she wanted, but she nodded and walked out of the room to go upstairs anyway.

Cole met her at the back door, looking appropriately chagrined. "I'm sorry I didn't tell you," He started to explain, only to stop when Aubrey put up her hand to stop him.

"You don't owe me an explanation, Cole," Aubrey told him. "I'm the one who gave us "boundaries" for the time being," She tried to look at him but couldn't, "so I can't fault you for dating other people." Oh, being an adult sucked right now!

Cole reached forward and cupped her chin with his hand, "I'm not "dating" Linda. She's been asking me out for months. Last week, before I met you, I finally said yes, knowing there was more on her side than mine," he gently pulled her chin up so she would see his eyes when he told her, "I should have told you, and I'm very sorry that I didn't."

His words made sense, but inside she was a wreck. For years now, she'd been the one calling the shots in her so-called relationships. Now, compared to how she was feeling with Cole, they were merely distractions in an otherwise solitary existence. She didn't like that he could provoke these feelings in her either. But, that wasn't his fault, it was hers. "Okay, I'm sorry I'm being a bitch about it."

Amazed, Cole's eyebrows shot up, "A bitch?" He asked her, "When were you being a bitch?"

"In my own mind," Aubrey mumbled, "when I was cursing you and Linda."

He chuckled now, she looked so cute when she was pouting. "I'll take your "bitch" status any day over Linda's tentacles." He smiled, trying to get her to smile, "The woman makes an octopus look inept."

Cole did make her laugh with his words. Stepping back, she motioned for him to come in.

As he passed by her, Cole snuck a quick kiss.

Fast on his way to forgiveness, Aubrey asked him, "Hey, what's Linda the octopus' last name?"

"Meyers," Cole answered, then asked, "Why?"

Shaking her head, Aubrey commented, "Should have known, no imagination with that plain name."

He laughed outright.


They sat at the bar in her kitchen, talking. She went back downstairs to get her cold food, and heated it up quickly in the microwave. It was still awesome!

The conversation was lighter this time, no talk of feelings or other people; as if they both realized they needed to make up for the misunderstanding.

"How did you come up with A.J. Sloan as your pen name?" Cole asked her.

Smiling, Aubrey told him, "Aubrey Jane is my first and middle name, and Sloan was just a dreadfully easier way of saying my last name."

Cole chuckled as he answered, "I'll bet."

Sighing, Aubrey explained, "You should have seen my publicist and agent when I finally got a deal, they were tossing around names like it was a contest. I just thought of something easy, and they both looked at each other, me, and then said, okay." She shook her head, "Sometimes I think people make things harder than they have to be."

Cole agreed and nodded. "So, are you really rich?" He asked her, wondering if she would be okay with him asking.

Instead of answering, Aubrey asked him in return, "So you're really a contractor?"

He got the point, "Got it," he answered and knew that was something she wasn't willing to talk much about. He couldn't blame her. Even her parents were asking questions these days. "I know," She told him, "It seems weird not to build some big mansion or close myself off, right?" She posed the question rhetorically. "I just don't want that kind of life, I want to be normal."

Placing his hand over hers, "Aubrey, I think the one thing you will never be, is normal," he said, and followed it with, "but that's the thing I find most attractive about you."

Looking into his eyes, and seeing the sincerity there, Aubrey melted, "I think that's about the nicest thing any man has ever told me," she smiled.

"We'll have to change that then," Cole replied, and leaned in to kiss her.

Knowing that kissing Cole was like taking a match to dry kindling, Aubrey pulled back and offered, "How about we walk down for a drink?"

It took Cole a second to figure out where she was referring too. When he did, he replied, "Sure."

So, they grabbed her purse and keys, locked the house, and walked the four blocks down to where they had dinner a couple of nights prior, B.J. Wentkers.

Since it was Friday, the place was pretty packed. Cole must've known someone though, because he sent a text as they were walking over, and there were stools available at the bar when they went inside. Aubrey didn't question it, she just appreciated his efforts.

She ordered another Amaretto Stone Sour, blended, and he ordered a beer.

"Is that all you order?" Cole asked her, remembering that she'd ordered it the other night as well.

Aubrey tilted her head, as if she was deciding whether to answer the question or not. "For now, yes," She finally answered, "but I've been known to indulge in a nice glass of wine too." Nodding toward his beer, Aubrey asked him, "Is that all you order?"

He had to quit asking questions that she could turn back on him. "Yep, pretty much," He sighed, "but I have been known to indulge in a nice glass of wine too."

Him repeating her answer, felt like a dare. It was thrilling, their verbal back and forth. It made her feel that talking to him was worth her time. Good conversation, no matter where you lived, was difficult to come by. And Aubrey could never turn one down. "So, how did the lovely Linda wear you down?"

The only thing going through Cole's mind was Mine Field, after being asked that question. Although, he did think that the only reason Aubrey asked was because she was curious by nature. "She'd been asking me out for months, and I just kind of said, okay." He took a sip of his beer, "It was more like, let's just get this over with."

Aubrey actually felt sorry for Linda. She suffered from unrequited feelings and that was no fun. Thinking about feelings turned her thoughts to the letters they found in the floor board, so she turned the conversation in that direction, telling Cole, "I've been reading those letters that we found, and I'm going to the library tomorrow to try and do some research."

That got Cole's attention. "What kind of research?" He asked her.

"The kind that gets me answers," Aubrey replied, feeling confident that she would be able to figure out this mystery.

Lifting his glass, Cole waited for her to touch hers to it, and toasted, "Here's to figuring it all out."

He couldn't have said truer words, to Aubrey's way of thinking. She smiled and took a healthy drink of her cocktail, sighing as the cool liquid settled in her tummy, and made her head fuzzy.

Three drinks later, Aubrey was feeling a great deal more than fuzzy. She was afraid she'd embarrass herself if she drank anymore so asked Cole if they could go.

They were just about back to her house when she told him, "It wasn't that I wanted to leave, I was just getting too drunk, to be a lady."

Appreciating her candor, Cole returned, "Well, then we left when we needed to leave. I only kept it at one so I'm fine to drive home."

"Or you could stay?" She asked him as they turned down her street. Her house was only the second one from the corner so she left the question hanging between them until they got to her back door.

Giving her a kiss, Cole admitted, "If you just hadn't told me that you were just this side of being drunk, I might have taken you up on that."  He stepped back, "But I'll be here tomorrow, and we'll see what happens."

Aubrey stood at her back door as Cole left, her lips still tingling from his kiss and her head still reeling from his words.

## Chapter 13

Even though the next day was Saturday, Cole's team still worked. They had to take advantage of the warm weather months and were on a 6 day work week.

They were kind enough to wait until 9am to start work on the Duane Street house, but were noisy when they arrived. There were no donuts or coffee this morning, and no sign of Aubrey.

He sent the guys upstairs to start working on the joists, and he went downstairs to see if she was having some trouble this morning with drinking last night.

As soon as he came into the doorway, he stopped, the bed was empty. Checking the adjoining bathroom, she wasn't in there either. Her car was in the driveway, so he assumed she was here. Turning around, he was about to go back upstairs when movement caught his eye. Squinting, he looked to the far end of the family room, and saw that the fruit cellar door was standing open.

Strange, he thought, and walked over. Slowly opening the door, the creak of it filled the quiet and grated on his nerves. His stomach was tight, and fear clenched his chest. Even with the morning light, the room was dark, the only window at the far side of the room, didn't give off enough light to see clearly.

As he stepped into the room, Cole felt a cold chill embrace him. It was just like the other day, when he was going upstairs, only this time it was like cold hands clamped onto his arms and the sensation made him shudder.

When his eyes finally adjusted to the dimness, he saw Aubrey, sitting on the rocking chair. It was rocking gently back and forth, a lulling motion that did the exact opposite to his insides. "Aubrey," Cole spoke, his words sounding absorbed up into the darkness of the room.

He moved closer and saw Aubrey huddled into a ball on the chair, "Aubrey, honey," Cole said louder, but she didn't move. He stepped forward, the sound of his boots scraping the loose dirt as he walked.

The light coming on startled him, and he put up a hand protectively, before hearing Max behind him.

"Cole, are you okay?" The young man asked.

Now Cole could see clearly, and he turned and ordered Max, "Call her parents, the number is on my phone." He crossed the few feet to where Aubrey was balled up on the piece of furniture. As soon as he reached out, he felt her skin was cold as ice. "Baby," He murmured, "I'm going to pick you up now."

She made no sound, didn't move, and it scared the hell out of Cole. She was a slight thing, so he picked her up easily, and carried her out of the damp room.

As soon as Cole came out of the fruit cellar, he saw his crew, all huddled in the family room, looking worried. "Max," He shouted, "Are her parents on the way?"

Max's quick nod, made him feel slightly better. He told the guys, "Go on upstairs, and tell Dr. and Mrs. S to come down as soon as they get here."

Carrying the, still balled up Aubrey, Cole placed her down on the bed. "Baby," He kept saying softly, and finger brushing her hair.

Within minutes, her parents were there. Greg Slojankokowski had his medical bag with him, and examined his daughter, his wife right by his side.

"How is she?" Christine asked her husband.

Looking at his wife, worry on his face, Greg told her, "All her vitals are slow," he turned and asked Cole, "Has she said anything?"

Cole shook his head no, "I just found her in the fruit cellar, balled up on that rocking chair." He tried to remember, "Her skin was ice cold so I'm thinking she was in there for some time."

Greg asked his wife to go and turn on the shower in the adjoining bathroom.

After the water was nice and hot, Greg carried her into the room, but left so his wife could undress their daughter.

Staring at the bathroom door, Cole asked her father, "Is she okay?"

Although his fatherly instincts were on high alert, he knew she was breathing and her temperature was coming back up. "She was almost hypothermic and I don't have the faintest idea what she was doing in that room."

"She's been waking up looking tired," Cole told him, and that gained him a stern look from Greg. "I, uh, I haven't stayed over, we just talked about it," He said quickly, to explain it to her father.

Greg nodded, accepting the explanation.

Both men waited a few minutes, until Christine came out. She closed the door behind her and walked over to sit on the edge of the bed.

"How is she?" Greg asked her.

Looking up at her husband, Christine was stumped, "Fine," she answered and threw her hands up in a helpless gesture. "As soon as she was in the water, it was like a switch was flipped." Christine looked at Cole, and asked him, "Did she tell you anything?"

He shook his head no.

Sighing, Christine told her husband and Cole, "I don't want her staying here, what if someone put her in there?" She asked, starting to panic.

Cole told her, "The door was open when I came down here," he didn't want to worry them, "I think she's just stressed out."

Christine got up, and was about to go back into the bathroom, when she spotted the pictures and letters spread out on the top of Aubrey's dresser, "What are these?" She asked Cole.

Stepping forward, Cole told her, "Oh, we found those under a floor board in the entryway the second day she was here."

Aubrey came out of the bathroom to find her parents looking at the letters and pictures she'd found upstairs. Cole was pacing the small space like an expectant father, and the thought of that made her smile. "I'm okay," She said loud enough for all of them to hear.

Cole turned and went to her, his hands gently clasping her upper arms. Even through her robe, she could feel the intense heat his touch created.

Her father came over to her, and guided her over to the bed and helped her sit down on the end of it. "Can you tell us what happened?" He asked his daughter.

Looking from her father, to her mother, and then to Cole, Aubrey tried to remember. "We went to the bar and had a few drinks," She looked at Cole. "Cole walked me home and left pretty soon afterwards," Her brow creased as she tried to concentrate. "I came down here, got ready for bed, was a little giggly from the alcohol, and fell asleep quickly." She leaned into her mom, who now sat down beside her on the bed. "I kept dreaming," She felt a headache coming on because she was trying to jog her mind. "There was a voice," She said, "crying out."

Tears were now streaming down her face, and Aubrey had no idea why. She just felt a deep sadness come over her.

Christine hugged her daughter closer. "I'm not sure what's going on here, but maybe you should be at our house?" She asked Aubrey.

"No," Aubrey told her mother in a serious voice.

Greg crouched down so he was face to face with Aubrey, "Sweetie, we're just really worried about you."

Now Aubrey turned her face to Cole, pleading with her eyes for him to help her.

Cole clapped Greg on the shoulder, "Why don't I stay here with her while we're working on the house?" He asked her parents. "I'll stay in the next room, or upstairs, but I'll make sure nothing happens."

Standing up, Greg turned and looked at Cole. He'd known this young man long enough that he knew Cole would honor his word. Looking down at his daughter, he didn't want to leave her here, but it was her house and she was an adult. "Okay," He said, and received a glare from his wife.

This whole thing was being blown up, Aubrey thought. "Listen," She said to her parents, "Mom, Dad, I promise that nothing like this will happen again."

Christine wanted to believe her daughter, but they didn't really know what happened in the first place, so how could she be so sure nothing like it would happen again.

Cole left Aubrey to speak with her parents.

As soon as he got up to the main floor, he saw his guys milling around. Pasting a smile on his face, he told them, "Okay, excitement is over," he pointed upstairs, "Let's get this done for the client."

The guys reluctantly went upstairs and got back to work. Cole ended up joining them because he needed the distraction of physical labor to keep him from wrapping Aubrey up in his arms and refusing to let her go.

A while later, Greg came up and asked if he could speak to Cole. They walked down the hall and into another bedroom.

"I'm not old fashioned," Greg told Cole, "I know my daughter is old enough to have relationships with whomever she likes," he was uncomfortable discussing this with Cole, "and we're friends so that makes this even more difficult." He finally gave Cole a small smile, "But

Christine and I would feel better if you stayed here; since it's clear our daughter won't leave."

Cole would like to think he understood how his friend felt, and nodded, "I'll keep her safe."

That's all Greg could hope for. He shook Cole's hand and told him, "We've convinced her to at least go out to breakfast with us, so I'm sure she'll be mad by the mother hen routine Christine is about to pull out."

Chuckling, Cole nodded, "I'm sure."

After Greg went downstairs, Cole went back to work. He started planning what he would do. The guys with the joists for the attic arrived, and the crew carried the large beams upstairs. It took several hours to get everything in place, but they did it. On Monday they could finish getting the electrical put in and do some framing for the new closet and bathroom.

He'd have his crew working in the other bedrooms, doing some drywall patching and removing the paneling from the bedroom at the top of the stairs.

When he called for the guys to break for lunch, they all came downstairs. His crew told him they were going out to get a bite. Cole nodded, and went downstairs to see if Aubrey was back from breakfast with her parents.

Sure enough, she was sitting at her desk, typing away as if nothing had happened. He waited for her to notice him before saying, "How are you doing?"

Not understanding any of what was going on, Aubrey told him, "I'm fine, really, it's like I just woke up this morning and everything was normal."

This whole thing was difficult to wrap his head around. "Any theories?" He asked her.

She nodded toward the letters, "I think it's her," she said, emotion invading her words.

Cole came in and sat down on the bed, when she joined him, he wrapped his arms around her. "Do you believe in that stuff?"

"You mean in ghosts or spirits?" She asked him. When he nodded, she shrugged, "I think I believe something is going on, and I need to figure it out."

Cole squeezed her again, and kissed her forehead before saying, "I'll help in any way I can."


The rest of the day, Cole worked with his guys, but took breaks often, so he was able to go down into the basement to check in with Aubrey.

After the crew cleaned up and was gone for the day, he went down, and suggested they order in a pizza. Aubrey agreed so he called a local place.

While Aubrey waited for the pizza to be delivered, Cole went back to his own house to pick up some things. He'd worked all day so he desperately needed a shower, but he'd just have to take one at Aubrey's house so he wasn't gone any longer than necessary.

He picked up enough clothes for a few days, grabbed his travel toiletry bag, and was out the door within twenty minutes.

By the time he arrived back at Aubrey's place, the pizza was delivered, and she'd opened up a bottle of wine. She smiled when he came in, and said, "One glass, to calm my nerves, and then I'm done."

Cole smiled, replying, "You don't need my permission, we're in your house."

Inside, Aubrey was relieved. She'd spent the majority of the day trying NOT to think about what happened and how she ended up in that fruit cellar. Now, with the night settling in, she was getting edgy about it happening again. Of course, she didn't want to admit that to Cole, but she sensed he wouldn't judge her if she did confess her fears.

They sat at the breakfast bar, and talked about the pizza mostly. Cole asking her about her life in California, and what was the biggest difference between living there and here.

"I guess," She answered, "it's the pace," she set down her wine glass and told him, "everyone there is in such a hurry all the time, honking and yelling for everyone else to move."

He understood what she meant because he'd been in Chicago during college.

Sighing, Aubrey admitted, "But the conveniences were nice, the variety of stores and services." She sat there dreamily for a minute or so before confessing, "What I wouldn't give for a Saks Fifth Avenue," she said with a sigh.

Her comment made him laugh, as it was meant to. "I'll see what I can do," He told her and they finished their pizza.

## Chapter 14

As they walked downstairs, Aubrey wondered what Cole was going to say. Neither of them really said anything except that he was going to stay. In an attempt to keep herself from being nervous, she asked him, "Do you know if the library is open tomorrow?"

Shrugging, Cole answered, "I don't think so, but we can look it up online."

They walked through the family room, and into Aubrey's room. She sat down at the computer and looked it up. "Nope," She told Cole, "they're closed on Sundays."

Cole smiled at her, "Well, then we'll just have to do something else."

Puzzled, Aubrey asked him, "Like what?"

Tapping her nose with his finger, he replied, "I'd like it to be a surprise."

All Aubrey could do was smile, and nod in agreement. When he was like this, a ruggedly handsome gentleman off the movie screen, she was simply helpless to resist him.

Feeling the shift in the atmosphere, Cole cleared his throat. He'd promised her father he'd look out for her, not seduce her. "Uh," He looked around the room, "Do you want me to get out the air mattress and bunk out in the other room?"

Aubrey stood up, and framed his face with her hands. "You'd do that wouldn't you?" The question didn't require an answer, they both knew he would. She didn't wait for him to respond, just leaned in and kissed him.

Her kiss was like a drug to Cole's system. Everything inside of him settled down, and accelerated up at the same time. The contradiction of feelings made his head spin, and his arms came around her. If he wasn't so damn worried about her, and about what her parents thought, he'd probably say to hell with the consequences and make love to her right now.

As soon as Aubrey felt Cole start to pull away, she tightened her hold on him. "No," She said, "stay with me here, in my bed."

Oh, she had no idea how those words tormented him. "I think…" Cole started to say, but was silenced with her kiss.

"Don't think," Aubrey told him. "We won't make love, I just want to touch you."

Those words did absolutely nothing in helping his lustful thoughts settle down. He leaned his forehead against hers, and whispered, "I'll do whatever you need."

Raising her eyebrows, Aubrey's mind came up with some pretty descriptive things that she probably "needed" right then, but now, tonight, was not the time for them to take their relationship to that level. Tonight was about intimacy of a different kind. "Okay," She answered him, and turned to go into the bathroom.

Cole watched her go into the bathroom and close the door behind her. Now, he could take a deep breath. Holy cow, the woman had no idea what she did to him physically or emotionally! He went back upstairs to grab his bag.

Brushing her teeth, Aubrey tried not to be nervous. She wasn't some teenager, she was a successful, and experienced woman. So why did she feel giddy and anxious?

She brushed her hair, and slipped into her oversized t-shirt, realizing that she hadn't brought any other clothes into the bathroom with her. When she came out, Cole was nowhere in sight. Quickly grabbing a pair of old shorts from her dresser, she tugged them up so she at least appeared to be covered. She heard him then, coming back down the stairs, and sat on the edge of the bed, feeling the nervous energy pulse through her.

The house was locked up tight, Cole saw to that, and made sure all the lights upstairs were off. His crew had a habit of leaving a window or door open in their rush to leave for the day, so he went up to the second story as well, just to make sure everything was secured. When he was assured it was, he went back down to the basement and found Aubrey sitting on the edge of the bed; looking as nervous as he felt. Thank goodness, he thought to himself. At least it wasn't just him then. He had his bag in his hand and nodded toward the bathroom, asking Aubrey, "Do you mind if I change?"

She shook her head no, looking almost shy.

Cole went into the room, which was actually more spacious than he originally thought. His contractor's eye looked for imperfections, as was the case with every house he ever went into. He took a quick shower, and then changed into his "pajamas," which consisted of a pair of basketball shorts and white t-shirt. Not sexy by any means, but they were comfortable. He brushed his teeth and came out of the bathroom, only to find that Aubrey was still sitting in the same place. "Are you okay?" He asked.

"Nervous," She replied in a cracked voice. Then laughed because she sounded so unlike herself.

He crouched down in front of her, taking her hands into his, and asked her, "Why?"

Aubrey rolled her eyes, "Because," she dropped his hands and stood up. "Every time I'm near you I get all weird inside, like I just want to throw everything out the window and get crazy!" Anger built up inside her then, as she saw him smiling, "It's not funny!"

Finding it funny that he was actually the calm one right now, Cole went to her, "It's not funny; it's sweet." He said softly.

"Okay," She glared at him, "You know how guys hate to be called "Nice?" Well, women hate to be called "sweet." It makes it seem like we're not very sexy."

His smile gone now, and replaced with want, Cole looked her in the eyes, and said, "Oh, Aubrey, I think you underestimate your sexiness."

Still pouting, Aubrey mumbled, "I've never really been known as the woman who was sexy."

Tipping her chin up with his hand, Cole told her, "And yet, it's all I can think about when I'm around you, go figure."

It was a scary and thrilling thing, hearing a man tell you he wanted you. Aubrey smiled.

"Now, which side of the bed do you sleep on?" Cole asked, trying to make light of a potentially explosive situation. "I prefer the left, but I'll compromise since it's your place."

Seeing Cole acting as if they were negotiating a contract rather than figuring out sleeping arrangements lightened Aubrey's heart. He was making this easy and she was the one getting all riled up. The least she could do is be dignified about it; he was doing her a favor after all. "I like the right," She told him, and they crawled in.

It was only a full size bed, so if either of them thought they would have any distance, they were wrong.

Aubrey giggled as Cole tried to be a gentleman and hug his side. "It's okay if we touch, right?" She asked, trying to sound innocent, and knowing he didn't buy it for a second.

He moved his arm up so she could nestle into his side. Her arm was wrapped around his chest and her legs were touching his. Cole wasn't sure if he'd get any sleep because she felt so damn good against him, but he tried to be still in order to let her relax.

Placing her head on Cole's chest, Aubrey felt safe….. safer than she ever had before, and sleep lulled her into its comfort within minutes.

As soon as Cole felt Aubrey's breaths slow and knew she was asleep, he allowed himself to follow.

The next morning, Aubrey woke up in the exact same position she'd fallen asleep in, her body snuggled up next to Cole's. The only difference was that now, his other hand rested on the arm she laid across his chest, as if he were holding her in place, even in sleep. There were no unshed tears in her eyes today, no feeling of being exhausted, and obviously she hadn't moved in the night. It was sheer bliss to feel the security of him next to her.

Unfortunately though, she had to use the restroom, and with the bed being so small, there was no way she could get up without waking him. With a resigned sigh, she started to move.

"Good morning," Cole said in a gravelly voice.

Smiling, Aubrey looked up into his eyes. They were still sleepy but he had the most beautiful smile touching his lips. And, she was pretty sure he was the most handsome man that lived. "Good morning, yourself, I'm sorry I had to wake you but I have to pee."

A chuckle shook his ribs, "Okay," he answered, and let her go.

There was a chill in the morning, but Aubrey hadn't wanted to use the furnace since the days were warm enough. She ran to the bathroom and jumped when her feet his the cold linoleum, she yelped, and then jumped again when Cole was in the bathroom doorway asking her, "What's wrong!" His face was flushed with worry. She looked at him, feeling sorry that she scared him, and answered, "Cold floor."

Cole dropped his head in relief, chuckled, and left the room, closing the door behind him.

Aubrey started up the shower and went through her morning ritual. She hadn't thought to grab clothes, not smart, but Cole was more than a gentleman about the whole thing. It wasn't easy for her, so she concluded that this wasn't easy for him either.

While Aubrey was in the shower, Cole ran upstairs to use the "water closet." It was funny to stand in a closet and pee, but you had to do what you had to do. He came out, and washed his hands at the kitchen sink.

As he came back downstairs, he heard Aubrey rustling around the bedroom, "Are you decent?" He asked before turning the corner to entering the room, and laughed at her reply of, "Physically or mentally?" Assuming that was a yes, he turned the corner into the bedroom and stopped in his tracks. She had only a towel wrapped around her body, her hair looked towel dried, but still stuck to her shoulders in wet clumps.

"Sorry," Aubrey rushed, "I was trying to grab clothes.

Using every trick he could, mostly repeating "baseball, baseball, baseball" in his mind, Cole nodded and went into the bathroom to get ready while she got dressed.

Ten minutes later, he came out, dressed, thanks in part to leaving his bag in the bathroom the night before. "All set?" He asked Aubrey.

Dressed, and ready to go, Aubrey didn't understand, and asked him, "For what?"

Cole walked over, pulled her up from the office chair, and informed her, "For our adventure, of course."

Smiling at him, Aubrey just nodded, and let him lead her upstairs, and out the back door.

Their adventure started with breakfast at a little diner downtown. It was a family style place and, since it was Sunday, was filled with families either going to, or coming from church.

They each ordered a big breakfast platter, which included eggs, bacon, sausage, diced potatoes, and even pancakes. Aubrey looked at the food with skepticism.

Cole laughed and told her, "You can do it, just dig in."

The meal was good, and Aubrey did do it justice, which surprised both her and Cole.

As they talked over coffee, she said, "Thank you again, for staying over last night."

"How did you sleep?" Cole asked her, before taking a sip of his coffee.

Her eyes wide, Aubrey replied, "Awesome!" She leaned forward and whispered, "You're better than Mr. Bear."

Intrigued, Cole asked her, "And who is Mr. Bear?"

Aubrey sighed, "Well," she started, "Mr. Bear was the absolute best teddy bear a girl could ever have. He was my most trusted companion from the time I was eight until I left for college."

Cole made a slight bow, and said, "High praise then." He smiled, "Thank you."

"To be compared, in any way at all, to Mr. Bear is tantamount to being knighted," Aubrey said with a very straight face.

Smirking, Cole announced, "Then I shall be called Sir Cole of the Night Guard."

Aubrey bobbed her head back and forth, as if considering his title. "I think that's pretty good," She told him, and smiled.

When the server brought the check, Aubrey snatched it first, and got a nasty look for it from Cole. "I don't care," She told him, "I am repaying you for last night."

Without a missing a beat, Cole told her, "Letting me hold you in my arms all night was payment enough."

And there it was, Aubrey thought to herself, those words he used that made her feel as if she were the only woman in the world. Her chest was throbbing with awareness. It was difficult to breathe when he was making her feel this way.

It didn't escape Cole's notice that she didn't respond to his words. He knew they hung between them, stretching the chemistry between them more tightly. There was no way they would last the week without making love if he stayed at her place. There was too much of a connection between them. He wouldn't call himself a believer of a lot, but he did believe that there were things you couldn't, or shouldn't fight against. What was between them, this tangible connection, was one of those things. So instead of being flippant or pushing her, he simply left it. And when they got up to leave, Cole made sure he was touching the small of her back as they walked out to his car.

# Chapter 15

Twenty minutes later, they were driving out Hwy 11 West. Cole made so many turns onto different roads that it wasn't long before Aubrey didn't know where they were. All she did know, was that late spring in Wisconsin was greener and more beautiful than she ever remembered. They had the windows down, the smell of fields and cows drifted in and out as they passed farms.

"Where are we going?" Aubrey asked him a few minutes later.

Glancing over at her, Cole answered, "Nowhere, not yet at least."

The answer was just what Aubrey hoped for. She leaned back and enjoyed the scenery as the green fields, dotted with red barns and white farmhouses passed by. Eventually they ended up on a back road that led to the nearby town of Lake Geneva. Mainly a tourist destination, Lake Geneva had a street of shops that provided a diverse selection of items, from one-of-a-kind designer purses to home goods, to fresh ice cream, and everything in between.

Cole parked on the main street that was still made out of cobblestone and they got out. The sun was bright, making everything look sleepy and peaceful.

They wandered along the sidewalks of the town, going into any shops that happened to catch their interest.

Cole encouraged Aubrey to try and find some accent pieces
of furniture or some design element for the house. It was a
two-fold mission; it kept her mind off the strange goings on
at the house and kept her with him. He loved her smile; the
way her whole face lit up when she found something she
thought was special.

Hours later, their arms loaded with small bags,
Aubrey looked at Cole and said, "I'm hungry."

He winked, and told her, "I know just the place."

They walked back to the car, loaded the bags into the
trunk, and were off.

When Cole pulled into the parking lot at the Dairy
Queen in Burlington, Aubrey gave him a skeptical look.

He chose to ignore her cynicism and drove around to
the drive thru lane. When it was his turn he told the clerk,
"Two hot dogs, ketchup, mustard, and 2 chocolate shakes."

Looking at him, Aubrey commented, "A little high-
handed of you to just assume I wanted both ketchup and
mustard on my hot dog, much less a chocolate shake."

Cole tried not to laugh, "A correct guess, I'll wager."

She sneered, then nodded reluctantly, saying, "Yes,"
which made him laugh.

After getting their order, Cole drove down the road and turned into a parking lot. He grabbed the shakes, and asked Aubrey to get the hot dogs.

Following Cole into a wooded area should have made Aubrey nervous but, instead, it made her curious.

They walked behind a large fence. If you didn't know where you were going, you wouldn't notice the narrow path that led along the Fox River. They walked for about ten minutes, weaving through the brush, and finally coming up on an old, deserted railroad trestle.

There was nothing around them, at least that you could see, and Aubrey got the impression that they were all alone. It was peaceful, watching the river run beneath you and to see all the trees. Since spring was in full bloom, the trees were lush with leaves.

Cole sat down first, hanging his legs off over the side of the trestle, he took the bag from Aubrey so she could join him.

That's where they ate, sitting there, watching nature. There was a family of squirrels across the river, playing in the trees.

"What do you think of my secret place?" Cole asked Aubrey, in between bites of his hot dog.

Smiling, Aubrey answered, "Well, it's definitely secluded, and very pretty," she added. "I love it!"

He was glad that he could make her smile, and nodded. "And dinner?" He sighed, "Is it okay?"

After thinking for a few seconds, Aubrey replied, "Dinner is great, but the scenery and the company are awesome."

His heart skipped a beat. "Well, then," He said, and pulled his phone out. Looking through the music, he picked a song, and pressed play.

The area seemed to come alive with the music. The notes echoed off the trees and reverberated back to where they sat. It was almost magical, Aubrey thought. She looked over at Cole, who was drinking his shake, and thought he was about the most simply complex man she'd ever met. "I think you probably impress all the girls with this place," She said teasingly.

Giving Aubrey a confused look, he told her, "I don't bring girls here."

His tone was serious and Aubrey felt she'd put her foot in her mouth once again. Why did she just assume things where Cole was concerned, when he clearly wasn't like any other man she'd ever met? He didn't pressure her to be someone she wasn't, he didn't expect things from her, he just let her be herself, and that was the one thing she'd always struggled with, figuring out exactly who she was. "I'm sorry if I've upset you," She said quietly.

Cole knew she didn't mean to say things that stung, "I know," he reassured her, "I'm just different I guess."

"Funny," Aubrey smiled, "I was just thinking that I'm different and I've always struggled with that."

Nodding Cole responded, "Well, maybe we both just needed to find the other person who was as different as we are?"

Unsure what he meant by the question, Aubrey didn't want to read into it. Of course, if he was saying that they were meant for each other, that was what she thought. If he was referring to a "friendship" she'd never turn it down, but she knew she wanted a lot more with Cole.

They sat on the trestle for a while longer, just enjoying the music, mixed with the sounds of the birds, the breeze rustling through the leaves of the trees, and the small animals who occupied the area.

Cole suggested they head home when the sun started to dip low. Aubrey nodded, and finally checked her phone. Her jaw dropped when she realized it was early evening already. She had no idea how long they were there, only that she'd missed several calls from her mom, one from her agent, and two from friends in California.

When they got back to the house, Aubrey asked Cole if she could have some privacy to return the calls. He told her he needed to go to his house and check things anyway, so that was fine.  After leaving her house, it dawned on him that he really just needed some distance from her.


Aubrey called her mom first, "Hey, Mom," she said when her mother picked up.

"Where have you been?" Christine asked her daughter.  She hated using the tone of a worried mom, but she was worried.

Smiling, Aubrey was thankful that her parents cared enough to check in on her.  "Cole and I went into Lake Geneva and then picked up some dinner."

Christine stopped pacing, and answered, "Oh."  She didn't really have anything else to say.  Cole was there and her little girl was safe.  "How about dinner sometime this week then?" She asked Aubrey.

"Sure," Aubrey replied, "I'll check with Cole and call you in a day or two."

Giving her husband a look, Christine only nodded, and then said, "Okay, love you."

Aubrey answered, "Love you too, bye," and hung up.


Christine Slojankonkowski plopped down in a chair next to where her husband sat, her face blank.

Greg knew that lack of any expression meant that his wife was perplexed by something. "Are you going to tell me, or do I have to guess?" He asked his wife.

"She's in love with Cole," Christine answered, finally realizing she'd just verbalized her thoughts.

Nodding, Greg shrugged, and said, "Good."


The call to her agent was the one Aubrey dreaded. Her publisher had emailed, wanting the first 3 chapters of her new book and she'd barely gotten 1 chapter done. It wasn't like her to miss deadlines, and she truly felt bad about it, but none of the things that had happened were planned.


When Cole returned to Aubrey's house, he didn't bother knocking, just went in. As soon as he heard her raised voice though, he ran downstairs. She was yelling at someone, and he'd yet to hear her all worked up like this.

"Sharon," Aubrey wasn't calm, she didn't want to be calm, and she wasn't going to be, "I'll damn well have the book to you by the deadlines!" She paced the bedroom. "Have I ever been late? In the last ten years, have I ever let you down?" There was silence while she waited for the answer, "Right," she shouted, "so don't start doubting me now, I've made you a hell of a lot of money and I'm not

going to tank my career because of what you call, a crazy
move to find my roots!"

Cole smiled when he heard those words. He also
knew that he didn't want to be on the receiving end of her
anger so he would need to watch himself. Clearing his
throat, so he wouldn't scare her, he poked his head inside
the room.

Aubrey was relieved to see Cole, she motioned for him
to come in, and told her agent, "I'm hanging up now,
Sharon, I'll talk to you on the conference call on Tuesday."

After she pushed the disconnect button, Aubrey let
out a breath. "Lord," She said to Cole, "that woman is
strung tighter than a nun's butt!"

Laughing at her joke, Cole asked, "Are you behind on
your work?"

There was no use in lying, he'd obviously heard
enough of her conversation to figure it out. "Yes, for the
first time in ten years, I'm a little behind."

As someone who worked with deadlines himself, Cole
could understand the frustration. "Is there anything I can
do to help?" He asked her.

Smiling, Aubrey walked over to him, wrapped her
arms around his chest, and said, "You already are." She
kissed him quickly, then released him. "I'll be back on
track tomorrow and then they can kiss my ass!"

Again, Cole mentally reminded himself not to get on Aubrey's bad side. He winked at her, and asked, "How about a movie?"

Aubrey stopped moving, and gave him a blank stare, before saying, "I don't have a television or a DVD player."

Cole laughed and announced, "Well then, we'll just just have to go to the store and remedy that situation."

The rest of the evening was spent picking out electronics, with Aubrey letting Cole make all the decisions. It may have been for her house, but she had no interest, whereas Cole had some sort of electronics genius knowledge that he was more than willing to share.

By the end of the shopping excursion, Aubrey was the proud owner of a 60 inch, high definition television with surround sound, and a DVD/Blue Ray player that did all sorts of stuff on the internet.

If she thought Cole knew his stuff at the store, he really proved himself useful when setting up the pile of electronic devices. In practically no time, he had it all set up in the family room of the basement, since that's where it would most likely stay, and they laid on the air mattress to watch movies.

It was the best day that Aubrey had experienced in years.

## Chapter 16

Monday morning, Aubrey was up early, she even beat Cole, who normally was up by 5:30am. When she saw him get up with his alarm, she'd been up writing for a good 30 minutes. The smell of the coffeemaker from upstairs, also a purchase from the store the night before, wove its way down to them.

"Good morning," Cole muttered as he woke up. He'd slept well, but they'd gone to bed late after watching a movie and his body wanted to stay in bed, with Aubrey beside him.

Pausing her typing, Aubrey turned to him and smiled. When she was writing she needed very little sleep. It was like the story took over and she was in its grip. "Good morning," She returned, and asked "it smells like the coffee is done so do you want me to get you some while you try to wake up?"

Not fully conscious yet, Cole merely nodded.

Smiling, Aubrey got up and stopped to run her fingers through his hair as she passed him. She was humming when she got out some cups to pour the coffee into. Before she could pick up the carafe to pour the hot liquid, she started feeling dizzy.

*All of a sudden, the room spun and looked completely different. The cupboards, the counters, even the breakfast nook was different. She was standing at the counter, writing a letter. She could see her hands moving, with the pen between her fingers.*

Suddenly, she was back in her own kitchen, leaning against the counter and trying not to throw up. "Cole," She croaked out before sliding to the floor.

Cole was surprised when Aubrey wasn't waiting for him with the coffee when he came out of the bathroom. He went upstairs, his heart jumping out of his chest when he saw her sitting on the floor of the kitchen shaking. "Aubrey," He fell down to the floor in front of her, taking her into his arms, "What happened?"

Aubrey was still trying to figure out what happened, she couldn't wrap her mind around it. "I don't know," She whispered to Cole, her body starting to feel better. "I was at the counter, then everything in the room changed and I was here, but it didn't look like this," she pointed to the room.

"Okay," Cole said to her, "Now I'm starting to think your parents might be right and you should stay at their place or my place?"

Shaking her head no, Aubrey knew what was happening was happening for a reason. "NO!" She pushed herself up, refusing to talk about it further. She poured them each a cup of coffee, handed Cole his, and then went back downstairs to continue writing.


She didn't see Cole again for the rest of the morning. She heard him alright, banging around upstairs as if he was mad. Maybe he was, maybe he was mad because she was being stubborn? Taking a break from her writing, she sat back and stared at the blank wall in front of her.

The only good thing about all of this was that she was now ahead of schedule in her writing. The first four chapters of her new book were in an email to her publisher, and Aubrey felt like they were good. Developing her characters was the fun part of any book, seeing where they could take her, and maybe letting them have some freedom that she, herself, didn't have. "Enough!" She said aloud, grabbed her purse, and headed upstairs.

Although no one was on the main floor, there was nothing sounding short of chaos on the second. Someone had a radio turned up loud, there was shouting, and the sound of power tools went on and off in random rhythms.

Going upstairs slowly, Aubrey didn't want to get in anyone's way. She peeked into the master bedroom and found both Cole and Sean huddled over, what looked like, blueprints.

"Aubrey, my love," Sean said lightly, when he noticed her. He left Cole and walked over to her, giving her a quick hug. "I was just letting Cole know that everything looks good here."

Cole watched the other man, as he held Aubrey possessively in his arms, and wanted to punch him..... Very Hard...... in the face. Of course, he didn't do that, he pasted on his business smile and joined them, telling her, "The joists are in, the electrical is done in here, but we had the electrician look at some other parts of the house as well, just to be sure."

Aubrey nodded absently and looked around the room. It was so different! In just a few days, these men were transforming it into the sanctuary she desperately needed. "Thank you," She finally said to Cole, realizing that he was waiting for an answer. "I'm sorry to bother you, I just wanted to let you know that I'm going to the library to work on that extra project." The words were directed to Cole.

He nodded quickly, and strolled over to where one of his guys was working on the soon-to-be master closet.

Sean eyed up his new friend, "Trouble in paradise?" He asked, and winked.

Smiling, Aubrey answered, "Let's just say, we're trying not to mix business with pleasure too much."

Throwing his head back, Sean laughed loudly, drawing the attention of everyone in the room. He waved them off saying, "Mind your own bees wax!"

That made Aubrey laugh. Sean was a fun guy, "Uh, we mentioned lunch last week, do you have a day this week that works for you?" She asked him.

Leaning over, Sean kissed her cheek, and whispered, "Thursday, I'll pick you up or meet you there, and oh, Cole is getting so jealous with me whispering in your ear like this."

Aubrey slapped gently at his arm, and shook her head. She knew he was being intentionally naughty, but he was so much fun. If Cole was jealous, well then it served him right after that whole thing with the tentacle-clad Linda on Friday. She smiled sweetly at Sean, and turned to leave.

Cole stood by the window, facing Duane Street, and watched Aubrey pull out. She'd put down the top of her convertible, and the breeze was blowing her long, light brown hair behind her. He turned around, to get back to work, and found himself looking straight into Sean McAdams' eyes. "What's up?" He asked the man, not really wanting to talk.

Sean hadn't known Aubrey long, but he'd worked with Cole on and off over the years since they both moved to Burlington. He knew Cole was a man of his word, but he also knew the guy had women hanging on him like he was a tree limb, and they were the leaves. "I know you're not going to take this in the way I mean it, but don't hurt her."

Not knowing exactly how he was supposed to take that comment and letting his anger start to build, he asked Sean, "What do you mean?"

"She's a classy lady, Cole," Sean explained, "She's successful, beautiful, and has a good head on her shoulders."

Impatient with Sean's obvious comments, Cole asked, "I know, so?"

Sean cocked his head to the side, "So, don't hurt her," his tone was now more serious.

Cole looked out the window a moment before turning back to his associate, "Did it ever occur to you, Sean," he added, "not that this is any of your business," he glared at him, "that maybe the one in danger of being hurt is me?"

Standing there, Sean watched Cole go over to where his guys, who were starting to install drywall, were waiting for him. Honestly, the thought hadn't occurred to him and he was making a mental list of questions to ply Aubrey with when they had their lunch, in a few days.


Aubrey drove down to the Burlington Public Library, and parked behind the old building. There were as many memories here for her as any other place in Burlington. Some consisted of studying for tests or writing papers, but most were of combing through the shelves, trying to find the perfect book to read. She'd been drawn to the mystery/suspense genre long before she began to write it.

As she made her way up the walkway, Aubrey smiled. She couldn't help but be happy to be in a place where there were books. She only hoped she would be able to find out a little about the mystery surrounding her own house.

It was quiet inside, as it was in libraries, and Aubrey didn't see anyone at the reception desk right away so she popped over to the online reference area.

After sitting down, Aubrey pulled out her phone. She'd taken pictures of the pictures and letters, not wanting to lose or damage the originals. She started by putting in Duane Street, and Burlington history into the computer to see what she came up with.

There were a few books on Burlington, one actually put out by the Burlington Historical Society, so that's where she began.

Hours later, Aubrey was sitting at a table, pouring over pages of books when she was approached by a woman. The woman looked as if she recognized Aubrey, but was too embarrassed to say anything. Taking the situation in her own hands, Aubrey asked, "How are you today?"

The lady, replied, "Ms. Sloan, I'm Charlotte, one of the librarians here."

When people used her pen name, Aubrey drew the conclusion that they either didn't know her real name, very unlikely here with all the hubbub her mother created, or they didn't know how to pronounce her real name. "Hello," She said to the librarian.

"We're so excited that you're here," Charlotte said nervously, her hands clenched together, "If there's anything you need, you just let me know."

Nodding, Aubrey told her, "Thank you, I will," and went back to reading.

Twenty minutes later, she could still feel the eyes of Charlotte on her and knew she'd never get research done. Instead, she came up with another plan. Taking the books up to the counter, she waved Charlotte over. "I'm having some difficulty finding out some information on a house I purchased here," She told the woman.

Charlotte, looking very serious, would do anything that Ms. Sloan wanted, she was a super huge fan of the novels Ms. Sloan wrote, and the fact that Ms. Sloan was from Burlington was a very big source of pride for Charlotte. "Well," She told the younger woman, "You could try City Hall, I believe they have all the tax records for the properties."

Smiling, Aubrey leaned in and whispered, "You're a Godsend!" Making the other woman blush.

Aubrey ended up applying for a library card so she could check out the books that she found. As soon as she finished with the ever-pleasant Charlotte, she darted across the street to where the City Hall offices were located.

The office was small with several desks behind a large counter. Not sure who she should ask for, Aubrey just used the little bell that had a sign saying "Ring for Service."

A smiling woman walked up and asked Aubrey what she could help her with. Aubrey explained that she was looking for history on her house. The clerk asked for the address then asked Aubrey for a check or money order for ten dollars, and said the information would be available within the next two days.

Feeling somewhat let down, at not getting the information she wanted, right away, Aubrey decided to go home.

She ran back to the library parking lot, and remembered that the Historical Society was just kitty corner from it. But, her hopes fell when she walked over and realized the building was only open on Sunday afternoons.

Aubrey walked back to the library parking lot, got into her car, and pulled back out onto E. Jefferson Street.

Within minutes she was home, and the guys were bringing stuff outside and putting it in a large dumpster that now occupied the back part of her driveway.

She got out of her car, and asked Cole's foreman, Zeke, "Is it okay if I park here?"

Zeke nodded, but added, "I'd make sure you parked closer to the street though, he looked over and nodded toward the guys, "Sometimes they aren't really accurate when throwing things."

There was a shouted, "Speak for yourself," that came out of the house and made both Aubrey and Zeke laugh. Aubrey got back in her little convertible and backed it up so it was just shy of the sidewalk going down the street.

When finally got inside the house, she was amazed. The carpet was pulled up off of the stairs, there were tarps thrown over the banister upstairs and all the way down the stairs, she assumed to protect the wood. It was starting to look like they were really getting messy. She jumped when she heard Cole behind her asking, "Are you sure you want to stay?"

Cole knew she hadn't seen him or heard him come up behind her. He'd long since worked off his frustration at her insistence on staying here in the house, and knew they would be done with the master suite in a little over a week if they kept on schedule. The removal of the paneling in the 2nd bedroom was proving to be a bit more of a chore than they thought. Whoever added the room didn't follow building codes so there were some hiccups in that area. The other two rooms just really needed paint and to have the windows re-sealed and the floors re-finished.  He was taking every door in the place, stripping it down, and putting a maple wood stain on them to match with the original look of the house.

He wanted to tell her all of this, but the words wouldn't come out.  Instead, he stepped forward, took her face in his hands, gave her a gentle kiss, and let her go so he could rejoin his crew upstairs.

"I'm fine right where I am," She called after him.

Aubrey knew then, that she was in love with Cole Rafferty.

## Chapter 17

At five o'clock, Cole sent the guys home, and told them they'd done a great job. He didn't let them know he was staying here, at the house, but knew they'd find out soon enough. The thing with small towns, and Burlington was still considered a relatively small town, was that your secrets didn't stay secrets for very long.

He went downstairs, to find Aubrey typing away on her computer, bobbing her head in time with some music. At least, that's what he hoped she was doing. "Hey," He waved his hand to catch her eye, and smiled when she pulled off the headphones she was wearing. "How's it going?" He asked.

Aubrey smiled, "It's good, editor likes the first four chapters, yay me!" She beamed. "I'm hungry, do you want to grab some dinner?" She asked Cole while she saved her work and shut down her computer.

The woman's ability to change subjects so quickly was mind-blowing. Cole did catch up and nodded, before asking, "Sure, as long as you don't mind if I use your shower first?"

"Sure," She told him, and stood up to go upstairs. She wasn't sure she could trust herself knowing that Cole would be naked and only about eight feet away from her. When he shut the door to bathroom, she made her way upstairs to the second story.

"Wow!" Aubrey said when she entered the room. She'd have to give Cole's guys a big bonus, they were immaculate. Even in the middle of tearing things down and building things up, there wasn't anything on the floor to trip over or step on.

Aubrey heard Cole come up behind her a few minutes later, but didn't turn around. "You're making my dreams come true," She said softly.

Wrapping his arms around her waist, Cole pulled her to him slowly. "Is that what I'm doing?" He asked, smiling into her hair, "I thought I was just renovating your house."

Leaning back into his strong chest, Aubrey sighed, and said "It's the same thing."

They stood there, looking at everything in the room for a few minutes before Cole whispered, "Didn't you say you were hungry?" He felt her nod, and stepped back, taking her hand to lead her downstairs.

Aubrey drove tonight, wanting to feel the wind in her hair. The nights were getting warmer as April made its way into May. "Where are we going?" She asked Cole as she pulled out of the driveway."

"Zumpano's" Cole answered, "It's in the loop."

Knowing where that was, since she'd just driven down there the previous week, Aubrey nodded and headed toward State Street.

The trees were blooming, thanks to the spring rains, and the streets were now surrounded with the wooden sentinels, protecting the houses from the winds and giving privacy. The one thing Aubrey didn't miss from California was the decidedly small amount of trees that seemed to grow there due to the development of the state. Here, the trees were big monuments of time, there, they were last minute additions to make something more appealing to a buyer.

And there it was, the smell Aubrey had been waiting for......Chocolate! "Ahhh," She said, and smiled.

Cole chuckled, "Never get tired of that, for some reason," he offered.

"I'm a woman," Aubrey mentioned, "so I'll crave it."

He laughed, and placed his hand on her thigh. It wasn't meant to be intimate, but his touch caused her skin to prickle with excitement.

A few minutes later, she was able to find a parking spot, and they walked into the restaurant.

"Cole," A voice called out. A medium built man, with glasses, came over, "How have you been?" He asked Cole.

Smiling Cole returned, "Great, Ralph." He motioned to Aubrey, "Ralph Zumpano, meet Aubrey Slojankonkowski, or as some people know her, author A.J. Sloan."

Ralph smiled, and said, "Welcome, please have a seat." Before scurrying off to somewhere.

They found a booth in the corner, and made themselves comfortable.

A waitress, who introduced herself as "Tasha," gave them glasses of water and asked if they wanted anything from the bar. Aubrey declined but told Cole, "You're more than welcome to indulge since I'm driving." He smiled at Aubrey, and asked Tasha for a soda.

As they looked over the menus, Aubrey relaxed. Writing relaxed her, but in a completely different way. Here, with Cole, she didn't think about work, the house, the crazy things going on in her life, she only had to focus on what to eat and stare at this gorgeous man.

He put down his menu, and Cole sat there, watching Aubrey watch him. "Did I miss a spot when I showered?" He asked jokingly.

Aubrey leaned forward, placing her head on her palm. "Nope," She told Cole, "I just like looking at you."

Mimicking her, Cole responded, "I think I like looking at you more."

She was about to dispute it, when Tasha brought over their salads. The goo-goo eyed discussions would have to wait in order for her hunger to be appeased. Afterwards though, she'd make sure she made him hurt.....just a little.

Dinner was great, they talked about Aubrey's research on the house and her new book. She described her new characters to Cole and he seemed genuinely interested. That was kind of unusual since most people looked at her like she was nuts. She always told people that writing was the only job in which it was acceptable to have other people inside your head. He laughed at her characters' antics, and asked great questions.

They were considering their dessert options when Aubrey's phone went off. Looking at the caller I.D., she saw it was Jess. "Do you mind if I take this?" She asked Cole, who nodded and said "Sure."

"Hey, Jess," Aubrey greeted her high school friend.

Jess smiled at Aubrey's greeting, the girl was always upbeat. "Before you say no, it's done," She started. "We're all meeting up at B.J. Wentker's on Friday to see you."

Smiling, Aubrey asked, "Who's we?"

Not giving up anything else, Jess replied, "You'll have to show up and see, Friday, about eight."

Jess didn't even give Aubrey a chance to reply before she hung up.

Cole sat there, looking at a very perplexed looking Aubrey, and asked her, "Is everything okay?"

"Lord, I hope so," Aubrey replied, and told him what Jess just told her.

"Sounds like fun," Cole said.

Aubrey nodded, but always had mixed feelings when thinking about her friends from high school. She was one of those kids that wasn't really popular, but had friends from all the main social groups. Some people would probably say she was nerdy and others would say she was a goody-goody. "Why is it?" She directed the question to Cole, "When you know you'll have to see people from high school you get nervous?"

Smiling, Cole replied, "Oh, I don't know...... maybe because high school is the most socially awkward time of your life and those people either helped you cope or made you miserable."

Her eyebrows raised, Aubrey nodded, and said, "Yep, you're right."

They left that topic alone and focused on dessert. The restaurant was known for their cheesecake so Aubrey ordered a slice for her and Cole to share.

Tasha served them the plate, with two forks, and they dug in. Aubrey saying, "Ooooohhh, this is soooo good!"

Cole loved watching her when she was happy. He'd never met a woman who could so easily be pleased and it was thrilling for him when she just smiled. "You are definitely the easiest woman to please," Cole said the words before he thought about how they might sound.

"Really?" Aubrey asked him. "How would you know how easily I can be pleased?"

The air was pulled from his lungs. He couldn't mistake the undertone of sexuality in Aubrey's words. "I'd love to find out," He replied, knowing he could dish it out as well as he could receive it.

Aubrey took the next bite of cheesecake, and slowly brought it to her mouth. Almost excruciatingly slow, she put the sweet dessert in her mouth and made a show of wrapping her lips around the fork. Seeing Cole swallow hard only urged her to tease him more. She closed her eyes and made a sound, "Mmmmmm," as she pulled the fork back out.

It didn't matter that Cole knew exactly what Aubrey was doing and what her intentions were as far as arousing him, he fell for it. "I suggest we go back to your house and see if I can prove my point."

Thinking for a moment, Aubrey shook her head no. She suggested, "I think maybe we should go to your place instead."

The thought resonated through Cole's brain and then went straight to his groin. "Okay," He gulped his soda, and motioned for the check.

If it wasn't so funny, she would have thought it was someone else who was going through it. He was adorably awkward and knew exactly what to say to put her at ease.

Tasha brought their check and Cole handed her his credit card without even looking at it. When she came back, he signed it, wrote an amount for the tip, and was standing up within seconds.

They walked out, waving goodbye to Ralph, with Aubrey complimenting the food and promising to return soon.

Since she was driving, Aubrey had to rely on Cole to direct her out to his place. He lived to the west of town, in the "boonies." It wasn't hard to imagine him here, when she pulled into the driveway he pointed out. It was an old farmhouse, like her parents' place. She thought it was adorable.

They got out of the car, and walked up the front stairs to the porch. Aubrey found herself feeling a little nervous as Cole unlocked the front door.

When they went inside, she gasped. The house may have looked like her parents' place on the outside, but inside it was completely different. "This is great!" Aubrey said as she walked slowly through the entryway.

The floors were all hard wood, and he'd kept the original configuration of smaller rooms. The difference was that he opened up the doorways into archways so it kept the vintage feel without making you feel closed in.

Cole gave her a tour of the main floor, showing her a study, a living room, a dining room, and a kitchen with an eat-in area. The kitchen was Aubrey's favorite so far. He'd left the original metal cabinet doors and drawer fronts, but he'd painted them a bright cherry red and put shiny nickel hardware on them.

Aubrey sat down at the 50's style table he put in the kitchen and gave him a look. "What made you pick this?" She asked him, nodding to the kitchen.

Sitting down across from her, Cole answered, "The house was built in the mid 50's and I didn't want to change the feel of it. He nodded, "You may not feel so warm and fuzzy when you see the room I use for my "Man Cave" downstairs."

Laughing, Aubrey retorted, "You've seen my joists and base boards and fruit cellar so I don't think there are many secrets between us by this point."

It was hard for him to keep a straight face when she simply made him want to laugh. "I think there might be some secrets we still hold."

Leaning forward, Aubrey asked him, "Why don't you show me some of yours, and then I'll show you some of mine."

His blood pressure pounding in his brain, started going south quickly, Cole stood up and offered her his hand, which she gave it to him without reservation. And that told him that this was right.

They walked upstairs, with Aubrey sneaking glances at the pictures he'd lined the stairway walls with.

His room was at the end of a long hallway. She saw glimpses of other rooms, but didn't want to stop for fear she'd chicken out. Not that she doubted she wanted to sleep with Cole, it was just that she hadn't prepared.

"Are you nervous?" Cole asked as they walked into his bedroom.

Looking around, Aubrey nodded. It was huge, and like her master bedroom on Duane Street, it was clearly two separate rooms at one time. His bed was like him, sleek and masculine. It was king-sized and done up with muted gray colors in the bedspread.

She was standing at the end of the bed when Cole stood in front of her, and took her into his arms, saying, "Tonight is not about houses, or books, or old friends; tonight is about you and me and us sharing our secrets."

When he said things like that, Aubrey was putty in his hands. "Okay," Aubrey whispered before he captured her lips with his own.

## Chapter 18

Cole wanted to take this slow. He wanted to savor her, body and soul, until they were both in ruins, physically speaking. He kissed her, his lips warm and tender against hers while his hand cupped the back of her head. He could feel the softness of her hair as it cradled in his palm, tickling the edges of his skin.

Aubrey knew he was taking his time, oh, but she didn't want it slow, she wanted him to completely overtake her. "More," She grumbled against his lips, putting her arms around his chest, and pulling him closer.

Could any man resist a woman who asked him for more? Cole didn't think so, and certainly didn't want to test the theory. He smiled, and opened his mouth to invite her in for deeper discovery.

Wanting to absorb him into her, Aubrey moved closer, they were front to front, kissing, touching, and exploring over the clothes. It was erotic and frustrating at the same time. She nipped at his bottom lip with her teeth, wanting to show him her intentions.

The quick slice of pain in his lip made Cole open his eyes. Hers were pools of deep blue, as if they were turbulent oceans. His hand slid upward and grabbed a fistful of hair in his hand and guided her head backwards so he could sample the skin of her neck. His free hand moved lower, sliding it up underneath her shirt. Her skin felt like velvet under his fingertips. He only stopped when his fingers brushed against the bottom of her bra.

Aubrey was grabbing at Cole's shirt now, loving the explosive need that was building in her. "Yes!" She ground out the words through gritted teeth while pushing herself closer to him.

This wouldn't be enough for Cole, he stopped and stepped back. She was breathing as heavily as he was, with her hair mussed, and those dark eyes, he smiled and picked her up into his arms.

Loving surprises, Aubrey smiled when he picked her up, as if she were nothing, and walked her around to the side of the bed. She knew he meant to set her down gently, as if they were in some old movie, but Aubrey didn't want that, she wanted mess and heat and crazy. She slid out of his hands and knelt on the bed in front of him, and reveled in the look of shock in his eyes. "No gentle, not tonight," She told him.

"Okay," Cole answered, and proceeded to follow through with her request.

He grabbed her, yanked her to him so they were pressed tightly together. The only constant contact was their lips, pressing, tasting, nipping, and exploring one another.

They each were grasping at clothing, trying to yank, pull, and get off shirts. Cole expertly reached behind her and released the clasp of her bra, with only one hand, which made Aubrey giggle.

They were both naked, from the waist up now, and Cole bent down to take her nipples into his greedy mouth. First one, then the other, he lathed them and made them pucker until he heard Aubrey panting with want. Her nails were digging into his shoulders as she held him to her, the exquisite pain making him want her even more.

He stood back up and was reaching for his belt when she put her hands over his, to stop him. "Let me," She whispered.

The transformation into this sexy vixen upped the need Cole had inside for her. Aubrey was the only woman who could sate his insatiable hunger. She slowly undid his belt and pulled it free from his jeans. Then, slowly, almost painfully so, she unbuttoned his jeans and slid the zipper downward. The sound of the separating metal echoed in the quiet of the room. He knew his hard shaft was pressing against his underwear, and he wanted to beg her to release it. Instead she ran the back of her fingers down the length of his arousal, and he dropped his head back to try and keep himself in check.

There was such power when a woman knew she had a man in the throes of passion. Aubrey wrote about it all the time, after all, she was human. But experiencing that

power, instead of writing about it, was intoxicating. "Touch me," She demanded of Cole.

Lifting his head back up, Cole smiled slyly. He placed his hands on her waist, and slowly moved them around her body until they were splayed on her lower back. He started kissing her again, occupying her mouth as his hands slid down below the waistband of her pants and cupped her bottom.

Desperation filled Aubrey's body, she wanted this man so badly. Pushing at the waistband of his jeans, and his underwear, she sighed when his hard shaft was freed and grabbed it to feel the silky length of it.

Cole felt his breath leave his lungs as soon as Aubrey held him in her hands. He wouldn't have thought this intimacy would be so comfortable, but he had no reservations about them, like this, and he felt like it was exactly right. He brought his hands around to the front of her pants, and undid the button and zipper, pulling down her panties along with the slacks. He moved away from her long enough to step out of his pants, and then he helped her lay down and remove hers.

Climbing on the bed, they lay face to face one set of hands clasped over their heads and the others free to roam each other's body.

"Make love with me, Cole," Aubrey said, and pulled him over so he was above her.

There were moments that you remembered in your
life, and Cole knew, Aubrey laying beneath him, opening
herself up to him, would be something etched into his
memory for the rest of his days. He positioned himself, and
entered her as slowly as he could, enjoying the look of
suspenseful energy she wore on her face. Even when she
tried to raise her hips, to make him go deeper, he pulled up.
"Patience," He whispered to her, and kissed her, his tongue
delving into her wet mouth at the same time his hardness
rushed into the wet heat she'd offered him.

As soon as they were joined, Aubrey's mind went
completely blank, she'd never felt such crazy excitement
being with a man. Instinctively, she began rotating her hips
to create more friction against him.

Cole pulled Aubrey's arms up, and held them above
her head with one of his hands. The other hand ran down
the length of her, touching and caressing as he started to
move with her.

Even though Aubrey was clearly no stranger to
intimacy, the heat and havoc making love to Cole created in
her made her body writhe in the sweetest agony. "Yes,"
She whispered, and smiled when Cole also whispered,
"Yes," in return.

They were going faster, each driving the other to go
further, to go deeper, and to reach the point of insanity that
only making love could bring to a body.

Aubrey screamed out, "Cole!" and felt the orgasm start to swell inside of her. It was if her whole body left its physical form and rose above them, hovering on another plane of existence.

"Yes!" Cole replied, and felt his own orgasm clawing at his insides. It was important that he keep hers going, so he held his off as long as he could.

Was it possible to have this kind of ecstasy drawn out until it wrung you out of all energy? Aubrey felt herself pull tighter, her body squeezing of its own volition, and when Cole gave in to his own rush of release, she experienced an intense heat through her belly that had her gasping for breath. It was the ultimate merging of pleasure and physical transcendence. Aubrey was pretty sure that what she experiencing was not just an orgasm, but something altogether different.

Cole fell down beside her, careful not to crush her with his weight.

They lay sprawled out on the bed, each of them trying to catch their breath.

Aubrey looked over at Cole, a sassy smile on her face. "That was amazing!" She told him, her words floating on a sigh.

Rolling over so he was facing her, Cole brushed her cheek with his fingertips, "Amazing is a pretty good word."

Winking at him, she commented, "I am a writer, you know."

"I know," Cole said, and pulled her to him for a kiss. This one, even though it kindled their desire, was gentle.

They fell asleep, nestled in one another's arms.

Sometime in the night, Aubrey woke up to use the restroom. She quietly went into the bathroom off the master bedroom and smiled at her reflection in the mirror. It was one of a woman thoroughly satisfied by a man.

She used the bathroom, washed her hands, and went back into the bedroom, only to find Cole sitting up, on the edge of the bed. "I'm not going anywhere," She told him, before straddling him, wrapping her legs around his body, and loving that her nearness was making him hard again.

Cole wondered how she knew what he was thinking. He experienced a moment of panic when he woke up to find her gone. He heard the noise in the bathroom and was going to get up when she came out. "You better not," He told her, and kissed her deeply.

Guiding Cole's hardness into her center, Aubrey felt the rush of excitement vibrate through her whole body.

And that's where they stayed, Aubrey moving back and forth, making love with Cole as they sat on the edge of the bed. Breaths mingled with moans and whispered promises. It was beautiful, the music that two people making love created. Aubrey felt her orgasm start to build and was determined to hold off for as long as possible.

Cole felt her hold back, and he grabbed her bottom again, pulling her against him with a hard desperation. "No," He told her, between kisses, "I want you to give me everything, no holding back."

His knowing her so well, so quickly, made Aubrey smile. "Yes, Cole, yes!" She yelled, and let the rush of emotions run over her. It was like being hit by a freight train, the momentum of the climax literally made her fall backward. Luckily, Cole was holding on to her and, even with his own release happening, kept her from falling onto the floor.

Gently, Cole laid her down onto the bed, her chest heaving with the vestiges of release still pulsing through her.

She groaned when he left her side, only to smile when she saw him lighting a fire in the fireplace. The heat of it, caught like the fire between them, quickly and spread through the room.

When Cole crawled back into bed, he snuggled in behind Aubrey, and pulled her to him. Nuzzling her hair, he told her, "You certainly know how to wear me out."

Aubrey giggled, "I think it's a mutual thing," she told him in return.

They didn't say anything else, only watched the fire in the fireplace until they both drifted off to sleep again.

*Aubrey was at the house, she was in the backyard again, and her heart was fluttering. He was there, she knew it. She always seemed to know when he was there. There was some internal piece of her that recognized the same in him and it was undeniable. She waited, while she watched the little girl, until he came to the window to look out. She gave him a quick wave, not doing anything else for fear someone might see. Her heart beat harder and she couldn't understand it.*

"Aubrey?" Cole asked her softly. He'd gone downstairs to get coffee going, and came back up to find her dreaming. She was mumbling, but he couldn't make out the words. Laying his hand on her arm, he tried to wake her gently, but had to jump back quickly, when she sat straight up in bed, looking frightened.

It was crazy! Aubrey thought to herself, this whole thing was nuts! How could she be having these dreams? "Okay," She looked at Cole, "I'm willing to see anybody, do anything, if it gets this to stop."

Cole was worried, and asked her, "What happened?"

Shaking her head, Aubrey couldn't remember everything, just bits and pieces, "I was looking for him," she said in a shaky voice, "and my heart, was just beating so fast when I knew he was there."

It didn't make a whole lot of sense to Cole, but none of this was making sense to any of them, from what he could see.

"We have to get back to the house before my guys," Cole said softly, and asked her, "Are you okay to get up and get going?"

Nodding, Aubrey tried to reassure him with a smile. It was a façade, she knew it, he knew it, but they both just had to figure this out.

Within minutes they were back in Aubrey's car, going to her place. Cole drove, wanting to give Aubrey some time to collect herself. He didn't ask anything because he had no idea what to ask. Up until now, he didn't even believe in ghosts or anything to do with the paranormal.

When they pulled into Aubrey's driveway, Cole turned off the car and turned to her, "Baby, you just go downstairs and try to rest for a little bit. I'll get the guys started and come down."

Shaking her head no, Aubrey told him, "Whatever this is, I have to figure it out, I'm not going to hide from it."

In the week he'd known her, Cole understood that she meant what she said.

## Chapter 19

Aubrey went downstairs and turned on her computer. She'd be damned if some ghost, spirit, poltergeist, or whatever the hell they called this, would make her afraid to be in her house. She yelled, "Do you see? I'm not going anywhere!" Her announcement was only met with silence, but Aubrey felt like there was now some understanding, at least on her part, and she got back to work.

There was something about having great sex that gave you energy. Aubrey was one of those people who didn't usually fall asleep afterwards, she was usually invigorated. Today was her deferred bout of energy after last night's activities.

She was knee deep in the sixth chapter of her book, a particularly gruesome scene that her detective character was going over, when her phone rang. It was her friend, Sahara, from California.

Sahara was a self-proclaimed psychic and Aubrey loved that about her. Sometimes, the woman was actually very accurate with her predictions.

"Hey there," Aubrey greeted her friend brightly.

In California, it was still early, but Sahara had a vision, and she had to share it with her friend. "You're in trouble aren't you?" She asked Aubrey.

Not understanding, Aubrey replied, "Uh, no, why do you ask?"

"She's not settled," Sahara said, reading her own notes from her vision, "I see a parallel love, one old and one new, and she needs you to help her."

Usually cynical, Aubrey's skin puckered up with goose bumps. "Who's she?" She asked her friend.

Sahara sighed, "I only see the letter M," she told Aubrey.

That was it! Aubrey started to cry, spilling out all the weird goings on since she moved into the house. It surprised her how emotional revealing this was, but Sahara was always a very good listener.

After hearing Aubrey's story, Sahara sighed, and told her, "Okay, I sense something bad happened and she thinks you can help."

All of this was a little much for Aubrey to take in, helping ghosts solve mysteries, it was more like something out of her books than actual real life. "I'll send you pics of the letters and photos," She told Sahara.

They spoke for a few more minutes, and hung up, each promising to talk again soon.

Aubrey had just put her phone back down on the desk when Cole knocked on the doorframe. "How's it going?" He asked Aubrey, a smile on his face.

Female pride filled Aubrey. She knew she was the one who made him look so satisfied. "The writing is good, but I just got the weirdest phone call...."

Cole's brow dropped, he walked into the room, and sat on the corner of her bed, waiting for her to tell him what was going on.

She did, she told him a little about her friendship with her, up until now, goofy friend from California named Sahara. She told him what Sahara said before she revealed anything that was going on here, and what she said afterwards. When she was done, she asked him, "Do you think he hurt her? Like physically?"

Shaking his head no, Cole answered, "I didn't get that vibe from the letters, but clearly something happened."

Dropping her head into her hands, Aubrey asked him, "Do you think I'm going crazy?" She looked up at him, "Seriously?"

Taking her hands, Cole rubbed them between his own, "Hell no!" He was adamant, "I saw you, in that room," he pointed to the fruit cellar door, "and I saw you upstairs on the floor, and I was scared."

His tone helped her. She needed someone to believe her, and clearly, Cole did. "Thank you, for believing me," She said to him. "Now, let's put this on the back burner for now, I've got a book to write, and you've got a house to fix up."

Cole smiled at her ability to compartmentalize things. It was actually very man-like, however that was about the only thing that was man-like in Aubrey. The rest of her was all woman.

For the rest of the day, Aubrey worked on her book, only taking breaks when hunger made her stomach growl, or she had to use the restroom. She loved it when she was consumed by her stories. They were her refuge from life, and it was especially nice when life was a bit tumultuous.

When Cole came down, at the end of the day, he found her in the same place, her fingers typing away, and her face lit up with excitement.

Instead of disturbing her, he decided a surprise might be in order. He left a note in the kitchen letting her know he'd be back, and went out to jump in his truck.

Two hours later, he returned, with a new grill and the makings for dinner.

He set everything up, and was happily out on the back patio, grilling steaks when Aubrey came out the back door. The surprised look on her face made him smile.

The smell of steak was strong enough to make it downstairs. Aubrey assumed Cole opened up the back door to lure her out of her little chamber, and it worked.

"That looks great!" She said and came out to give him a kiss of thanks.

The simple kiss turned into a series of kisses that kept Cole so distracted, he almost over-cooked the steaks. Laughing at his absent mindedness, he shooed Aubrey inside to pour them a glass of wine.

They sat out on the steps of the patio, eating steak with a salad, and wine. It was perfect, to Aubrey's way of thinking, although she did say, "I guess I need to invest in some sort of dining table."

"I thought you bought furniture already?" He asked, her, "You told me you'd ordered stuff from Roesing's."

Nodding, Aubrey replied, "Yes, but that's one of those fancy ones for the formal dining area, I was thinking something out here so we're not in the way," she pointed to the house.

Smiling at her, Cole said, "I'm up for a shopping excursion if you are."

Aubrey was certain she was about the luckiest girl in the world to find a man who actually didn't mind shopping. It was akin to seeing a unicorn in a female's world. "Okay," She warned him, "but don't say I didn't warn you."

Accepting her challenge, Cole finished the last of his steak, stood up, and offered her a hand, saying. "I think I'm up to it."


An hour later, Aubrey told herself to never underestimate Cole's mad shopping skills again. The man was a whiz! He actually pulled up sales ads on his phone and compared prices. Asking Aubrey a multitude of questions regarding what she wanted to have the table for, i.e. herself or for entertaining.

They left the store, a new outdoor dining set in the back of his truck, and Aubrey just staring at him.

"What?" Cole asked her, wondering what she found so fascinating about him.

Shaking her head in awe, Aubrey told him, "I'm just admiring perhaps the one shopper in the city of Burlington who could give me a run for my money."

Laughing at her teasing, Cole nodded, and answered, "You betcha, baby."

They chatted about her new book as he drove them back to the house. She told him how her character was chasing a particularly nasty bad guy who was sadistic.

"For someone who seems so sweet," Cole commented again, "these books of yours are pretty grisly."

Aubrey nodded, "You know, it's weird, how we writers decide on what we write." She looked out the window, letting the scenery pass by for a few moments, "I have this friend who writes contemporary romance and she is a hopeless romantic."

Cole asked her a little more about her friends in California, finally asking her, "Do you miss them? Your friends in California?"

"Sure," She replied, "but it's different there you know. Everyone is so busy that finding a time when everyone can get together is really tough. Oh," She snapped her fingers, "would you like to go with me to that get together Jess has organized for Friday?"

Looking over at her, Cole reached across the seat and squeezed her hand, "I'd love to," he told her.

When they got back to the house, Cole offered to assemble the outdoor furniture she purchased. Happily washing her hands of it, she said, "Sure," and went inside to call her mom.


"Hey, Mom," Aubrey said when her mom picked up.

Christine smiled, "Hey yourself, how goes it over there in renovation land?"

Aubrey laughed, "Believe it or not," she said honestly, "I am pretty good about tuning them out. I've got eight chapters done on the new book and my publisher and agent have gotten off my back."

Nodding, Christine was cutting up vegetables for a salad when her daughter called, "That's great! And, what about those dreams?"

That was one of the reasons she called her mom, "I wanted to tell you about a very interesting phone call I got from a friend in California today." She proceeded to tell her mom about what Sahara said. There was no need to worry about her mom's reaction to any of this since her mother kept a very open mind and believed in a lot of things.

Christine was intrigued by the information. "Do you believe it?" She asked her daughter.

A part of Aubrey did believe it, she believed that something was going on and the information Sahara provided actually tied in with what she'd gleaned so far. "I want to, but it seems too far-fetched."

"Part of believing is a leap of faith," Christine reminded her daughter, "There are plenty of things I've seen, as a mother, as a nurse, and as a daughter, that I couldn't possibly explain."

Aubrey knew her mom was right. Maybe being away from her family for so long had made her cynical, or maybe it was writing, but there were simple things in life that were magical and you couldn't buy them, you were just given them as gifts and you had to accept them. "I know, Mom."

They talked a few minutes longer, with Aubrey telling her about the impromptu reunion on Friday. They were about to hang up when Christine asked Aubrey, "So how are things with Cole?"

She should have known that she wouldn't get off that easy, and Aubrey smiled, before saying, "They're good."

"I stopped by last night, just to say hi," Christine said, smiling, "and your car wasn't there, but Cole's truck was."

Seeing no point in lying, Aubrey told her mom, "We went out to dinner and then stayed at Cole's house last night."

Her mouth forming a silent "Oh," Christine winked at her husband as he came into the kitchen. "Well, I need to feed your father before he starts getting grouchy, we'll get together soon, and I love you, bye." She hung up the phone and told her husband what Aubrey just told her.

Greg chewed on the information. Although he sincerely liked Cole, Aubrey was his little girl and it was difficult for him to see her as anything else.

Christine understood her husband's dilemma, she didn't want their little girl to grow up, but she did want her daughter to find love. With Cole, it seemed she did. "I'm sure it's a poor substitute for feeling like you're losing your daughter, but I love you," Christine told him, "and, after dinner, I'd be happy to go upstairs and show you."

After being married for thirty-five years, Greg still got excited when his wife was in the room. When she gave him a proposition, he was in it to win it! Winking at her, he said, "It may take a lot though, I'm just warning you."

The teasing was well worth it in Christine's mind. "You got it, as long as you need it, I'll be there."

They both sat there, at the kitchen table, smiling.


Aubrey went outside to see Cole had assembled the table and was working on the chairs, a small toolbox beside him. "How goes the assembling process?" She asked him.

He turned around and smiled quickly, before returning to his task, "I'm on a roll, what can I say?"

"Better you than me," Aubrey grumbled.

Now, he stood up and walked over to her, taking her into his arms and kissing her. "What would you have done if I wasn't here?" He asked her teasingly.

Pretending like she was considering the question, Aubrey contorted her face for a few seconds, then answered, "I would have paid someone."

He laughed, and kissed her again. "I'll bet." He said, and went back to his construction.

Aubrey went back into the house, made sure it was all closed up, did a few dishes, and then went downstairs to work on her book.

She'd just walked into the bedroom, and stopped, shocked by what she saw. "Cole!" She screamed.

He was downstairs in less than a minute, standing beside her, demanding, "What?"

Pointing, Aubrey couldn't voice her shock. The room was a mess, the letters and pictures were scattered about, the bed linens were all over the place, the books she'd borrowed from the library were dispersed all around the room, and the dresser drawers were empty, their contents all strewn all over the room.

"What the hell!" Cole demanded.

Turning around, Aubrey looked into the family room, and yelled, "This won't help me help you!"

He knew who she was talking to, but he was still pissed. "Come on, the outdoor furniture can wait, let's get this stuff cleaned up."

Aubrey was putting her clothes back in the drawers when she turned to Cole, who was straightening up her desk, and said, "I'm really sorry."

Cole stopped his cleaning and looked over at her, his heart squeezing when he saw unshed tears in her eyes, "Baby, it's not your fault."

"Whose fault is it then?" She asked him.

That was something Cole couldn't answer. He finally had all her papers organized, and said, "I'll help you find out."

They did stay at the house that night, but they were both quiet.

Aubrey was up most of the night, wondering what other things this ghost was going to put her through. Personally she was tired of it. Of feeling somehow responsible for something that clearly happened long ago.

# Chapter 20

The next morning, Aubrey was working on her new book when she received a call from the records division of City Hall that her records request was in.

She went upstairs to let Cole know she was going to pick them up. He was busy, so she just asked Max to let him know she went out, if he needed her. Max nodded, and continued to paint the bedroom he was working on.

Aubrey drove downtown, and parked on Pine Street, across from the City Hall offices. She went inside, and saw the clerk she first spoke to. "Hi, I was just called and told my records request was done," She told the clerk.

Smiling, the clerk gave her an envelope, and turned around to go back to her desk.

Even though she only lived about six blocks from the City Hall offices, it was the longest six blocks Aubrey had ever driven. She hoped that the answer to her questions were in the envelope, but there was no guarantee.

As soon as she got out of her car, Cole was standing on the front stoop. "Hey," She smiled at him.

"Hey," He replied, "did you look?" He asked her.

Shaking her head in denial, Aubrey answered, "No, I wanted us to do it together."

They went inside and through the house. Zeke hollered out a question to Cole, which he answered as they continued to walk.

Once downstairs, Aubrey sat on the bed, with Cole beside her, and opened the envelope.

It contained all the tax records for her property dating back to when the house was built in the late 1940's. Not having any idea how to read the documents, it took Aubrey a few minutes to find what she was looking for. She stood up and grabbed a pad of paper and a pencil from her desk, and started to take down names.

Cole read off the names and she wrote them down. They worked their way backwards from now. Luckily, the house hadn't changed hands too many times so the list only consisted of about twelve names. Obviously, they could discount her because she hadn't paid taxes yet and they knew she wasn't the ghost.

Once the list was done, Aubrey neatly tucked the information back in the envelope and put it in her desk drawer.

She and Cole went through the names. The original owner was a man named Charles McIntyre. The tax records indicated that the house stayed in his name until the early 1960's. The next owner was a woman named Eileen Schultz. They went through the whole list and didn't find anyone with the name beginning with M or W.

Feeling defeated, Aubrey turned to Cole and said, "I guess I thought it would be easy, we'd find M or W and be done with this."

"Me too," He leaned over and kissed her. He wouldn't let them get discouraged. "We'll figure this out, I promise." Trying to lighten the mood, he said, "I know a Priest, a Pastor, and a Rabbi so we've got our bases covered if we need some Theological intervention."

Aubrey did smile at his suggestion. "Well," She told him, "If this ghost doesn't leave me alone, I may need all three."

Zeke called down the stairs just then, "Hey Cole, the electrician is done, and the City Inspector is here!"

He smiled at Aubrey and said, "Duty calls," before kissing her quickly and leaving.

Aubrey looked at the list again, hoping that something would just jump out at her. After a while, she sighed, and put it aside to return to her writing.


That night was quiet, as if whatever force was harassing Aubrey realized she needed a break. They watched Netflix on Aubrey's tablet, and ordered Chinese food in from a local place.

Aubrey told Cole about her last relationship, two years earlier. "He told me that I was a little too different than other women," She relayed to Cole.

He was shocked, and asked, "What the hell did that mean?"

Laughing at his look of disgust, Aubrey responded, "I guess me writing about gross crime scenes and liking Jimmy Choo shoes was just a little too much of a diverse lifestyle for him."

Aubrey had a way of looking at things and putting them into simple perspectives. "His loss," Cole told her, and hugged her, before adding, "My gain."

That comment did make Aubrey's heart squeeze, in a good way. She hugged him before relaxing back into the crook of his arm, "Yes, sir."

They watched some television shows that both of them happened to like. Even with the big screen in the other room, this was more comfortable.

At some point, they both fell asleep, and were peaceful in the comfort they'd found together.


Thursday was a busy one for Aubrey. The City Inspector approved the electrical upgrades the day before so Cole and his guys were now able to finish the walls for the new bathroom and closet in the master suite. She had a conference call with her publicist and staff about her upcoming book tour, and she had a lunch date with Sean McAdams.

After her successful conference call, with successful meaning that Aubrey was able to keep it under ten different stops; four in the Midwest, three on the West Coast, and three on the East Coast, she jumped into the shower.

Having lunch with Sean meant that she got to dress up. No shorts and tank top today; it was all Gucci skirt with a Vera Wang top, and her beloved Nine West heels. She put loose curls in her hair, and actually wore makeup. Stepping out of the bathroom, she felt every bit the confident business woman, and hoped Sean appreciated her efforts. Most women would probably think those efforts were wasted on gay men, but Aubrey knew better. If a gay man appreciated your appearance, you were golden.

She was just grabbing her clutch bag when Cole came downstairs. The moment he saw her, he stopped in his tracks. "Hey," She told him, and spun around, "How do I look?" She asked.

Seeing Aubrey like this, Cole wasn't sure he knew her at all. Gone was the girl who liked to tear up carpet, and eat at Dairy Queen; she was now replaced with a designer version of runway model. "Uh, gorgeous," He managed to say.

He was telling the truth, Aubrey knew that, but she also had a feeling that something was out of sorts. Glancing at her phone, she knew she'd be late if she didn't leave soon, and gave him a kiss, before heading upstairs. "Call me if you need me," She said as she walked out the back door.

Cole stood there, just watching her until Zeke came up and stood beside him, "Holy Cow! Why'd you let her go out like that?"

Shocked, even though he shouldn't be, that Zeke figured out he was more than friends with Aubrey, Cole gave him a furious look.

Putting his hands up, Zeke backed up, and said, "I was just saying…..."


Aubrey would've put down the top of her convertible, but since she'd taken great pains with her hair, she didn't want to risk messing it up. She and Sean were meeting at a fancy restaurant in a suburb of Milwaukee, for lunch. Aubrey pulled up and noticed she just made it on time. She hated being late.

The hostess showed her to their table, and Sean was already there.

"La dee da," Sean said appreciatively, when he saw Aubrey.

She smiled, knowing she'd down a good job.

Looking at their menus, Sean asked, "So how goes the renovations?"

"Good," Aubrey told him.

Smiling, Sean asked her, "And how goes the renovations on Cole?"

Without looking up from her menu, Aubrey informed him, "Nothing needed there."

Giving her a dry look, Sean sighed. "I want details, woman!"

She'd just bet he did. They didn't talk details but they did discuss a variety of subjects during their lunch. Sean was great fun and she finally asked him, "Why aren't you out?"

"I don't know," He answered, "probably because I spend my days mostly working around manly men and I don't want anyone to call me anything less than I am."

Giving him a sincere look, Aubrey informed him, "I don't think Cole would do that."

Sean nodded, "Cole is definitely a different breed of man but, let's face it, I'm as tough as any of those muscle heads, twice as good looking, and with ten times the fashion sense."

Aubrey laughed, "You are, indeed."

They finished their lunch, and decided to go to a nearby mall.  Aubrey sent Cole a quick text telling him she'd be delayed, and got an "I told you so," look from Sean.

They went to the mall and walked around all the big stores.  Aubrey didn't need anything, she just enjoyed the time away from the house, with her new friend.  Missing Cole though, she found herself thinking of him when she considered a new dress or shoes.

"You're in love," Sean said as they walked out of the store and toward the food court to get something to drink.

Looking trapped for a second, Aubrey thought she'd recovered fast enough, but she should have known better. Sean had a quick mind and an even quicker eye.  "Yes, I am," She finally admitted.

Instead of saying something flippant or teasing her, Sean only said, "Good."

Feeling like the time was right, Aubrey turned to Sean and asked, "And what if I were to tell you some things that were going on at my house," she paused, "of the supernatural nature?"

Stopping dead, in the middle of the mall, Sean gave her a glare, and demanded, "Spill it!"

He steered her to a table in the food court, ordered some sodas, and waited as Aubrey told him the whole sordid story.

Sean sat there, absorbed in what she was saying, like a little kid during story time at the library.

When she finished she asked him, "Well, what do you think?"

"Let me get this straight," Sean began, "You've fallen in love, you've got a ghost that keeps haunting you, and you've had a psychic friend tell you that you're linked, in some way to this ghost?"

When he said it like that, Aubrey thought it sounded crazy. "No," She corrected him, "She specifically said parallel love."

Sean sat there for a few minutes, pondering the information. Then he sat back and crossed his arms as if he'd had an epiphany, "Simple," he said, "you just need to let things work out between you and Cole, because apparently things didn't go too well when she was in love."

As crazy as it all sounded, Aubrey thought he might have a valid point. "But all this stuff she's doing, is making it more difficult for Cole and I," She told Sean.

"Is it?" He asked her, "Would Cole have practically moved in only after a few days if she wouldn't have pulled all that stuff?"

Sighing, Aubrey replied, "No, he would not have."

As if he'd just solved a puzzle, Sean looked smug, and told her, "There you go then."

They strolled around the mall for a little while longer, and then parted ways. Sean's office was nearby so he went back there, and prepped for a dinner meeting with a new client, and Aubrey went home.

She spent the drive wondering if what Sean was saying actually had merit. All of these "disturbances" did, more or less, push her and Cole together very quickly. Maybe the ghost, or whatever she was, knew something she didn't. But, if it wasn't a happy ending for her, Aubrey hoped that didn't mean that Aubrey and Cole wouldn't find their own happy ending either.

By the time she pulled into the driveway, it was almost 5:30pm and the guys were all long gone. Cole's truck was there, and she hoped he wasn't mad that she was later than she told him she'd be.

She walked into the back door, and stopped. Cole was at the stove in her kitchen, an apron on, and stirring what she assumed was a sauce of some kind.

When Cole saw Aubrey pull into the driveway he was relieved. He waited for her to get in the door before turning to say, "You're lucky, if my pasta would've been ruined, I would've been pissed."

He said the words so seriously, that Aubrey had to bite her lip to keep from laughing.  He was standing there, with his hand on his hip, and she couldn't help it, she started to giggle.

## Chapter 21

Dinner was fantastic, with Aubrey offering to go and pick up dessert. Cole declined, but thanked her for the offer. He took her upstairs to show her the progress they'd made on the second floor.

"It's so different," Aubrey told him as she spun around in the middle of the master bedroom. "Have you run into any other issues?" She asked him.

Nodding, Cole walked over to where they were going to put in the master bathroom. "We found some damage to the floor in this area which is probably why you have patches downstairs on the ceiling," He told her.

Aubrey nodded, but honestly hadn't noticed the patches he was talking about.

He pointed to the wall, "But we found some stuff on a wall when we started taking it all apart." He pulled out his phone and showed her pics he'd taken. "See here," He pointed, "It's like a child's growth chart."

Nodding, Aubrey thought it was neat, but didn't know what the relevance was. She looked at Cole blankly.

He blew up the photo, and handed the phone back to her, "See here," he pointed, "It says Maddie," he waited for Aubrey to look closer and then smiled when she looked up at him.

"Maddie," Aubrey whispered out loud. "Do you think she's M?" She asked him.

Cole nodded, and replied, "I don't know how, but yes, I think she is."

Excitement bubbled up inside of Aubrey. "Maddie," She said the name again, hoping it would somehow tie in with her memories or dreams or whatever it was she was having.

That night, Aubrey was laying in Cole's arms. They hadn't made love since the night at his house. It's not that she didn't want to, it was more like she didn't want to rub it into the ghost's face, if that made any kind of sense whatsoever.

When she fell asleep Aubrey dreamed again.

*She was being pulled upstairs, by a little hand. When she looked up, she saw a little girl. "Come on Maddie," The little girl said, "Let's measure." They walked into a room and the little girl stood next to the wall. Aubrey saw herself mark the spot at the top of the little girl's head. The little girl giggled and Aubrey woke up.*

The act of her sitting up woke up Cole, and he asked her, "Are you alright?"

Looking at him, laying in the darkness of the room, Aubrey smiled, "You're right, her name was Maddie."

The next day was Friday, and Aubrey was glad. She was excited to see who Jess had rounded up for the night's festivities.

She was a good girl and worked on her book while the guys were upstairs, happily banging away on God knew what.

They'd managed to have some of the crew come down to the main floor to start the prep work in the formal living room and make sure the screened-in porch was sturdy enough to support the patio they were putting on top of it.

Most of the time, Aubrey could tune the noise out, but then someone would drop something, or yell, and she'd be pulled out of her writing zone. She couldn't blame them, this was what she was in for when she decided to stay here during the renovation process.

When Cole came down, at the end of the guys' work day, she was relieved.

He could see the noise was starting to intrude on her work and suggested, "You know, you can go out to my place and write during the day if you'd like. It's not like I'm there."

He was sweet for offering, and Aubrey considered it as she got ready for their party at the pub.

Cole ran back to his house, to get a fresh bag full of clothes and check on things there, so she had some time alone. She thought about her dream/memory as she got ready. As if she was hit in the head with a baseball bat, Aubrey stopped blow drying her hair, and walked out into the bedroom.

She pulled the pictures out of the envelope and stared at them intently for a few minutes. The little girl, in her dream, this could be her, she thought to herself. The dream was more vivid than the grainy picture, but Aubrey felt that they were somehow gaining ground.

When Cole came back to the house, she excitedly told her about her discovery. He was glad, but did say, "We still need a timeframe or another name."

Even though Aubrey knew they still hadn't come up with it, she nodded, and wanted so desperately to find out what happened to this woman.


They made sandwiches for dinner, so they didn't go to the bar with empty stomachs, and walked over, just as they had last week.

As soon as Aubrey walked into the front door, there was clapping and some whoo hoo's shouted. Jess walked up to her and hugged her tightly. "I got a few people to show up," She told Aubrey.

A few? Aubrey thought more like a couple dozen, but she was happy. There were faces she recognized right away and a few that she had to be reminded of. One of her best friends, from freshman year was there. Dina was like a big sister to Aubrey and they laughed all the time back then. Squealing, they hugged one another and chatted for a long time about each of their lives since high school.

There was a live band, and they were nice enough to play some hits from the 90's so the crowd was ramped up.

She ran into one of the nicest guys she'd known during high school. Brett was his name. They never dated but traveled in the same circles here and there. She'd had a crush on him for most of freshman and sophomore year, but he'd had a steady girlfriend then so she never stood a chance.

Aubrey told him about the crush, to which he replied, "Well, dang, if I'd have known that you were going to be this beautiful and successful, I might've paid more attention."

Cole watched Aubrey get reacquainted with her friends. Tonight, he wasn't jealous, he was proud. He was proud that she'd asked him to come with her, to share this. She introduced him as her "guy" and that was enough. Boyfriend seemed too immature of a title and they weren't serious enough for any other labels yet, although, if he had his way, those would come, in time.

"Cole," Aubrey waved him over, "I'd like to introduce you to my high school friend, Kylie."

Kylie smiled, and held out her hand to take Cole's. "Well, if I'd have known about you a little earlier," She pointed to Aubrey, "you would've been off the market long before this one showed up in town."

Aubrey laughed, but knew she'd have to keep an eye on the sharp-tongued Kylie. "Kylie works for the local newspaper," She told Cole.

Cole nodded, and asked, "Maybe she has some insight about the house?"

Not having considered that, Aubrey looked at her friend, "I bought that Dutch colonial house on Duane Street."

Kylie nodded, "Oh, the old McIntyre house."

Her ears perking up, Aubrey asked, "Yes, how did you know about that?"

"This isn't just a pretty face," Kylie retorted, and winked at Cole. She turned to Aubrey, "Oh, I'm on the Historical Society board and there was a big scandal years ago with the McIntyre's."

Completely intrigued, Aubrey asked, "What kind of scandal?" as her eyes shot over to Cole's. He was just as absorbed as she was in what was being discussed.

"There was a big fire back in the mid 1950's, in Mr. McIntyre's factory," Kylie told them, "and then about two months later, he died."

Cole asked Kylie, "Is that Charles McIntyre?"

Kylie shook her head no, and replied, "No, it was his son," she had to think about it, then said, "William, I think."

Aubrey and Cole looked at one another and silently asked the same question, was William the mysterious W?

Giving Kylie a big hug, Aubrey said, "Thank you," to her friend.

Before they walked away, Kylie said, "Hey, Aubrey, you know his daughter is still alive and lives just outside of town."

The revelation had Aubrey standing still, she turned around, and asked Kylie, "Daughter?"

"Yes, Charles and his wife, Marion, had a daughter named Eileen," Kylie informed them, "She's Eileen Schultz now, but she's still alive."

As soon as Aubrey heard the name, she repeated it to Cole, "Eileen Schultz owned the house after Charles McIntyre."

Kylie, not having realized how helpful she was being, told them, "Yes, the house stayed in Charles' name until Eileen was twenty-five or something like that, then it reverted to her."

Pushing her luck, Aubrey asked Kylie, "Do you think you could introduce me to Eileen?"

Shrugging, Kylie said, "Sure," and smiled again at Aubrey, "I'm sure with you being a big time celebrity, she'd love it." Then Kylie looked at Cole, "And if you ever get tired of this one, with her money and good looks, you just look me up."

Aubrey knew her old friend was half serious, so she'd have to be careful not to let Cole go.

A few other friends came up and talked to Aubrey. Some she hadn't seen since high school and some, she'd at least been on Facebook with so she had some knowledge of what they'd been up to.

There was a debate with one of her girlfriends about why Aubrey wasn't invited to the ten year reunion.

"Hey we thought you wouldn't show up," Her friend, named Jenny, told her.

Aubrey's jaw went slack, "Are you kidding, I'd have come!"

Jenny smiled and hugged Aubrey, saying, I think you'll get an invite to the twentieth."

"I better," Aubrey called after her, as Cole came up to where she was standing.

Cole saw Aubrey was happy. He asked, "How are you doing?"

Tilting her head, Aubrey stared at him for a minute, before answering, "I've had a good amount to drink, enough to feel good and still stay upright," she leaned over and kissed him, "and I have more information on a possible lead to our mystery woman."

"And, how are you?" She asked him back.

Cole mimicked her, tilting his head to the side, and answering, "I haven't had that much to drink, but I think you're the most beautiful woman I've ever seen."

She wanted to be serious with him, but the alcohol made her feel silly, and she retorted, "Or, Kylie, if I don't watch my step."

He laughed, "Yes, I like to keep my options open."

Putting her arms around his neck, Aubrey gave him a kiss. "Well, don't clear your dance card too soon, Mister, I plan on keeping you busy for some time yet."

"Is that so?" He asked her, and swayed her slowly to the music, "Who says dance card anymore?" He asked.

Smiling at him, Aubrey answered, "I do."

They stayed at the bar for a couple more hours, meeting up with people Aubrey knew from high school. Jess seemed to have the inside track on where everyone was now and she'd done a lot of networking to set this up.

Aubrey hugged her again before they left, saying, "Thank you for this, Jess."

Jess brushed it off, saying, "It was no big deal."

Shaking her head no, Aubrey corrected her friend, "No, and we both know different."

Laughing, Jess smiled and hugged Aubrey once again, "It's hard to find friends and keep them, so let's not let this much time pass again."

"We won't," Aubrey told her.


Aubrey and Cole were walking back to the house, with Aubrey telling him about some of the people she went to high school. "One of them is a teacher, and replaced our drama teacher when she retired. That's just too weird."

He wasn't sure if it was the alcohol talking or Aubrey's generally good mood with seeing old friends. He imagined it was a nice mix of both. "I'm glad you had fun," He told her.

"Did you," She stopped and wrapped her arms around him, "Have fun?"

Brushing her hair back from her face, Cole looked into her eyes, and said, "Yes, I was with you."

The effects of the alcohol muddled Aubrey's mind enough that she couldn't be serious. She giggled, and told him, "I hope so."

They walked the rest of the way home, and when they opened the back door, Aubrey stopped.

Since Cole almost ran into the back of her, he asked, "What's up?"

Maybe she had drunk too much, but she turned to him and said, "It feels better in here."

Not quite understanding, Cole asked her, "What do you mean, better?"

"I can't explain it," Aubrey told him, "just that I feel like she knows we're on to something."

Cole didn't comment, but he did hope she was right.

# Chapter 22

The next morning, Aubrey awoke, refreshed. She had no hang over from the night before, which was a miracle, and she didn't recall having any disturbing dreams. The sunlight was pouring into the basement bedroom, and Cole was nowhere in sight. Thinking he must've gone upstairs, she got up and got ready for the day.

Aubrey could hear the sounds of the guys working, while she showered, and felt pride that her house would soon be a showcase. She'd have to invite her friends over when it was done since, according to her mom, a house filled with laughter was the best kind.

After getting ready, Aubrey checked her emails, and responded to those she wanted to. There was one annoying one from her agent pleading with her to do more appearances for the new book series. She did what she could and shut down the computer. There would be no writing today, today was about the other matter.

While she was walking through the family room, Aubrey saw that the fruit cellar door was ajar again. Odd, since she saw Cole make sure it was latched the night before.

Opening the small door, Aubrey looked inside. There was the rocking chair, in its usual spot. Standing there, Aubrey could only stare at the single piece of furniture and wonder why anyone would put it in a dark, damp fruit cellar.  As she turned to leave, Aubrey felt a flash of cold pass through her body.  Irritated, she said aloud, "I'm working on it, Okay?" to the ghost.

Cole was coming down the stairs when he heard Aubrey's voice.  "Working on what?" He asked, then stopped when he saw her near the fruit cellar door.  Crossing the distance quickly, he took her into his arms, and asked, "Are you alright?"

Touched by his tenderness, Aubrey answered, "Yes," she sighed, "She's just impatient."

Pulling Aubrey closer, Cole told her, "That's something that seems to be going around."

"Hmmm," Aubrey said as she nipped his ear lobe, "We'll have to see what we can do about that."

They were kissing right there, when they heard a noise behind them.  Cole lifted his head, about to snap at the person who interrupted them, when he saw Max at the bottom or the stairs, looking embarrassed.  "Uh," Max said, "Zeke asked me to come down and get you."

Aubrey smiled, and said, "Thanks, Max," in a bright tone.  She stuck out her bottom lip as if to pout, to Cole.

He gave her a look and left with Max, clapping the young man on the back to let him know they were okay.

Aubrey smiled as she went upstairs.  One of the guys must have brought donuts, because there was a mostly empty box of them sitting on the kitchen counter. She grabbed one and thanked the Lord that there was some coffee left over.

Still munching on her donut, Aubrey heard a text message come through on her phone. It was from Kylie, Aubrey smiled, and opened the message. All it said was, *Call me.*

Aubrey called her friend, and walked outside so she could hear above all the noise the guys were currently making. "Hey, Kylie, what's up?" She asked.

Kylie was at work, again, on a Saturday. The news, even in a small town, didn't stop. "I wanted to let you know, I spoke with Eileen Schultz this morning and she's willing to meet with you."

Excitement bubbled up in Aubrey's stomach. "Okay, when?" She asked in a rushed tone.

Nodding to another reporter, who was silently asking about a story, Kylie returned, "Today, if you're free," she signed something and handed it to her boss as she spoke on the phone. "Do you want me to go with you?" She asked Aubrey.

Aubrey had to consider the question for a few moments. Deciding to err on the side of caution, she told Kylie, "Thanks, but Cole will be with me."

Sighing, Kylie mentioned, "Well, when you're done with that man, you just send him my way."

Laughing, Aubrey replied, "I'll keep that in mind."

They hung up and Aubrey went back inside the house to find Cole. He was upstairs in the master bedroom, going over some stuff with Zeke, so she waited, looking around the still unfinished room. It was taking shape that was for sure. Woody was out there doing, what else, but putting up an intricate wood railing.

When Cole noticed her, he walked over. She was clasping her hands together, and told him, "She'll meet with us today, if you're up for it."

Doing some calculations, and looking at his watch. Cole hesitated a few seconds then said, "Hey guys, we'll cut out early today. It's too nice to be working. Go home, the afternoon is on me."

The guys didn't have to be told twice, they straightened up and were out the front door within fifteen minutes. Aubrey was impressed, and stared at Cole when they were all alone, once again.

"Give a guy a paid afternoon off, and he's outta here," Cole told her with a wink.

She felt kind of bad that he had to pay the guys for the afternoon just so they could go talk to someone who may, or may not, even have any information for them. "I'm sorry," She told him, a worried look on her face.

Cupping her chin, Cole looked into her eyes, and asked, "Do you think I care about that?"

Aubrey shook her head no, and whispered, "No," she sniffled, "and that's why it means so much to me."

Pulling her into his arms, Cole held her. He wanted her to be the most important thing to him today, tomorrow, and always.

They left a few minutes later, after Aubrey got the address in a text from Kylie.

In her car, Cole asked her, "Do you know what you're going to ask her?"

Honestly, Aubrey hadn't given this part all that much thought, which was unusual for someone like her. "Nope," She told him.

Within ten minutes, they were pulling into a long driveway, and making their way up to an old Victorian house. "This is beautiful," Aubrey said as they pulled up next to the house.

Cole nodded, "It is," and got out first. He opened her door for her and held his hand on her back as they walked up to the porch. Before they could knock, a brightly dressed woman opened the door.

"Hello!" The woman said with a smile, "You must be the writer friend of Kylie's."

Aubrey, not sure what to say, just nodded, and looked at Cole. He didn't look that sure about it either, but they went inside.

Smiling, Aubrey asked the woman, "Are you Mrs. Schultz?"

The woman laughed, and nodded, "That's me!"

Her laughter was infectious, and Aubrey laughed with her. "Okay then," She started to get excited, "Um, I live in the house your grandfather built," she explained.

"First of all, call me Eileen, I'm way too informal for Mrs. Schultz," The woman told them, and led the way into a parlor. The walls were covered with pictures, and Aubrey migrated toward them, scanning as she walked.

She saw that Eileen had tea service set out, and thought that was a big departure from the flamboyant woman who just greeted them minutes before. Her confusion must have shown on her face, because Eileen nodded toward the tea service, and said, "I know right," she shrugged, "and I guess some things are just so ingrained."

Aubrey sat down, but motioned to the pictures, "Do you like to travel?" She asked Eileen.

Nodding, Eileen replied, "Oh yes!" She looked dreamy for a moment, then seemed to return to the moment. "So, what did you two youngsters need from me?" She looked at Aubrey, and then to Cole.

Cole decided to speak up finally, "Mrs......I , mean Eileen," he corrected when she shot him a glance, "We found some pictures and letters in the floor board of your old house," he pulled out the envelope, "and we found your growth chart on the wall."

It was as if Eileen was taken back in time, her face split into the sweetest smile, and she looked like a little girl. When she saw the pictures, she gasped and tears ran down her cheeks.

Cole and Aubrey exchanged glances, and were considering leaving when Eileen finally spoke.

"I thought it was a dream, a lovely dream," She whispered.

Aubrey felt awful for making this lovely woman cry, so she rubbed her back and asked, "What was a dream?"

Pointing at the woman in the picture, Eileen merely said, "Her," in a whisper.

Getting worried about upsetting Eileen, Aubrey told her, "She's been coming to me in dreams."

Normally she wouldn't reveal such a crazy thing to someone she'd only just met, but Aubrey felt like Eileen

Schultz might just understand. "And you were in some of them."

Her hand raising to her mouth, shaking in the process, Eileen turned away for a moment. Cole stood up and stood next to her, trying to show support. She finally turned and looked up to him, smiling, and telling him he was, "A sweet boy."

When he sat back down, Eileen started, "You see, I didn't grow up in a happy home." She took a breath to steel herself against the memories. "I should correct that," She smiled at Aubrey, "I lived in a home where the people there weren't very happy."

Settling back in her seat, Aubrey rested her hands on her lap and listened intently.

"My father," Eileen said dreamily, "from what I can remember was a very nice, mild mannered man." She smiled at the memory, "He owned a factory in town and always made time for me."

Eileen's face changed then, "And my mother….." She looked disgusted, "was the unhappiest person I've ever known. I swear, the woman could make ice look soft with one glare."

Cole tried not to laugh at the dramatic flair Eileen used. But, he knew she was serious so he remained quiet.

"I remember this woman," Eileen pointed to the picture." She smiled, "I think she was my nanny."

Aubrey nodded, "Her name was Maddie," she looked at Cole, "we think."

Eileen took a minute to roll the name around her mind, and nodded, "Yes," she said, "Yes, that's it, that was her name."

She smiled again, and told the youngsters, "Oh, she would play with me and teach me things. We would talk about faraway places," She leaned in as if letting them in on a secret, "But never in front of mother."

Again, Aubrey and Cole exchanged a quick glance, and turned back to Eileen, Aubrey asking, "Do you know if Maddie and your father were in love?"

"I was only five," Eileen answered, "I never noticed that, but it would make sense."

Cole asked her, "Why would it make sense?"

As if coming out of a fog, Eileen looked at him, and revealed, "They had a huge fight, mother and father, just after Maddie disappeared." She frowned, "I remember because it was on Christmas, just after the fire at the factory."

Aubrey couldn't even take it all in. She started making notes on her phone, about the fire, about it being Christmas. She didn't want to forget a single detail, in case they needed more information to help search the city records.

A tear slid down Eileen's cheek, "A few months later, Father was gone," she told them, "and I was sent away to boarding school."

Aubrey's heart broke for the woman. Her home was practically shattered, she lost her nanny and her father, and was pushed away by her mother. How awful! "I'm so sorry, Eileen."

Taking a deep breath, Eileen shook her head no, "Don't be dear," she tapped Aubrey on the nose with her perfectly manicured nail, "I found love. After I graduated from high school I moved back home." She wore a smug look, "And I met the love of my life, Jim Schultz." Again she seemed like she was telling a secret. "I was eighteen so Mother could do nothing about it, of course," She shook her head at the absurdity, "It didn't, however, stop her from taking credit for the marriage and making our wedding a circus. But Jim and I, we were in love. We have four children, ten grandchildren, and two great-grandchildren. God rest his soul."

Cole was relieved that Eileen was able to find some semblance of happiness.

Feeling bad about dragging up bad memories, Aubrey asked her, "Do you think there was anything bad that happened to Maddie?"

Taking a deep breath, Eileen replied, "I would love to tell you no, dear, but with Mother, one never knew." She shook her head again, "I didn't even let her see our children, not that she wanted to. I'm afraid I've always been a disappointment to her."

"Seems to me," Cole told her, "that your mother was the disappointment."

Smiling, Eileen leaned over and kissed his cheek.

She walked them out a few minutes later, saying, "I've enjoyed our chat," she kept the photos and the letters, bringing them up to her chest, "and I'll cherish these."

Nodding Aubrey asked her, "Please keep in touch and come to the house warming party when the house is done?"

"I will," Eileen replied, then asked them, "You know, do you want to ask Mother about all of this?"

Aubrey and Cole were about to get into the car, when they both stopped, and looked at Eileen.

"Your mother is still alive?" Cole asked.

Eileen nodded, "Yes."

# Chapter 23

For the next couple of days, Aubrey retreated into her work. It was easier than existing in the present, with the constant questions of what happened to Maddie plaguing her.

She only ate when Cole brought something down to her, and forced her to eat. Even when she wasn't writing, she was going over plot lines for her next books in the series, and was quiet.

By the third day, Cole was at his wits end and actually called her parents. Greg and Christine came over, under the pretense of checking on the progress of the renovations.

Greg went upstairs with Cole while Christine went downstairs, to talk with her daughter. When she saw Aubrey, her heart sank. Instead of being in love and happy, Aubrey looked almost despondent. It was gut-wrenching. "Sweetie," She said as she went over to where Aubrey was seated at the desk. "When was the last time you ate?" She asked.

Aubrey looked up and saw her mother, and smiled, "Mom," she said, absently finger brushing her hair, "I didn't know you were coming over."

Giving her daughter a questioning look, Christine told her, "Um, Cole," she pointed upstairs, "told us that he asked you and you said okay."

Vaguely remembering the conversation, Aubrey nodded, and replied, "Oh, yes, that's right."

By that time the men came downstairs, Christine was seriously concerned about Aubrey. She stood by, frowning, as Greg and Cole both tried to engage Aubrey into some semblance of a conversation.

Aubrey finally gave them an excuse of a headache, and they left her alone, the three of them going upstairs and outside to talk.

"What the hell is going on with her?" Greg demanded of Cole.

Putting up his hands, Cole answered, "You know as much as I do at this point." He looked at the house, then back to Aubrey's parents. "We went and saw the granddaughter of the man who built the house. She told us about Maddie, the woman Aubrey's been dreaming about."

Christine's eyes widened, "So she was real?"

Nodding, Cole explained, "I guess she disappeared the night there was a big fire at the McIntyre factory."

Greg looked at his wife, and then to Cole. "When did Aubrey start acting like this?" He asked.

"The day after we met with Mrs. Schultz." He answered, "You see, her mother, Mrs. McIntyre, is still alive and Eileen, er, Mrs. Schultz offered to get us an appointment to see her."

Thinking this whole thing was crazy, Christine began pacing. "All this talk of dead people, fires, the stress of moving, her writing......Greg," She looked at her husband, "Maybe she's having a breakdown."

Greg shrugged, "She's showing signs of depression, but I don't know," he answered.

Cole spoke up, "I'll tell you what, if we don't hear from Mrs. Schultz in the next few days, about meeting with Mrs. McIntyre, I'll let you know."

They agreed, and left. Cole waved as they pulled out of the driveway. His guys were now on the main floor, with only Zeke and Max doing the finishing work in the master suite. He had to figure out some way of getting Aubrey out of this funk.

When he went back in the house, he went through the main level, checking to make sure it was all locked up. By the time he got to the basement, he found the door closed, and locked. Knocking, he called out, "Aubrey?"

Aubrey was sitting on the stairs, on the other side of the door. She'd heard the whole conversation between Cole and her parents. They thought she was nuts! She wasn't nuts, she was just focused. "Go away, Cole!" She yelled through the door.

"Baby," Cole replied, "I can't do that, you know that. I am here to make sure you're safe."

"Safe from what?" She yelled, and threw open the door. She stomped up the last two stairs and pushed him backward. Her hands on her hips, she said, "You think I'm crazy, you all think I'm crazy!" She practically screamed.

His hands up, between them, Cole tried to remain calm, "Sweetie," he tried to think, "We don't think you're crazy, we are just worried because you're not eating or sleeping right."

Pushing him backward into the breakfast nook, Aubrey yelled, "Who the hell do you think you are?" She pushed him again, "I've been taking care of myself for years and now you think you need to babysit me? Besides, I told you, when I'm writing, I get distracted."

Anger was replacing worry, "You know what?" He shouted back, "You want "alone time," I'll give it to you!" He grabbed his keys and left, slamming the door behind him.

After Cole left the house, Aubrey crumpled into a pile on the floor of the breakfast room. She sobbed until she had nothing left to cry out, and fell asleep. When she woke up, the house was dark. She got up and felt like she'd been beaten up, she was so achy.

Flipping on the light, she went downstairs. The door to the fruit cellar was ajar again. "Okay," Aubrey yelled into the empty room, "I'm not going to put up with anything from Cole, so I'm sure as hell not going to put up with anything from you!" She slammed the door, and made sure it was latched. "Now, if you don't mind, I would like to get some sleep, and I swear," She pointed to the ceiling, "If anyone gets into my head, I WILL have a nervous breakdown and you'll never get the help you're demanding!" Having said her peace, Aubrey went into the bedroom and slammed the door shut.

The next morning, Aubrey woke up to the sound of power tools.......and she wasn't happy.

She should have known that Cole wouldn't stop working on the house even if she kicked him out of her personal life. He was a good guy, actually, he was a great guy, and she'd treated him like crap. Feeling guilty, she decided to call Sean and see if he had an available shoulder to cry on.


Cole had quietly gone downstairs to check on Aubrey when he arrived in the morning. She was sleeping, it looked like peacefully, so he closed the door and went back up as quietly as he could. Figuring the noise the guys made couldn't be helped, he tried to focus on the work. They were out in the screened porch, doing a face lift on that, while one of his subcontractors was redoing the fireplace in the living room.

He was out on the porch, when Oliver came out and said, "Hey, Cole?"

"Yeah," Cole answered absently, while he was holding a reinforcing two by six for Max to nail in.

Oliver walked over to him, and said, "The guy working on the fireplace found this," he told Cole and handed him a locket. "Said it had been in there for a long time by the looks of it."

Cole took the locket, and said, "Thanks," to Oliver. He went into the kitchen and found a clean cloth in which to try and wipe it off. He examined it as he wiped it, noting that it was old. Very carefully, he opened it up, and smiled. Taking the piece downstairs to show Aubrey, he was about to knock on the door when he noticed it was already open. Peeking inside, he saw that the room was empty. Since the bathroom door was open too, he was able to see that she wasn't in there either.

Just to be safe, he even checked the damned fruit cellar, but she wasn't in there either. Going upstairs, he peered through the kitchen window and saw that her car was gone.


Aubrey did leave the top down on her convertible this time when she drove into South Milwaukee. Her hair was pulled back in a ponytail so the wind wouldn't mess it up too badly.

She was getting out of the car when she saw Sean getting out of his, and walking over. "Well, well, look what the cat dragged in," Sean said sarcastically, then added, "Or should we say what the ghost dragged in?" and winked.

"Ha, ha, you're too funny," Aubrey responded in a dry tone. "Let's have lunch," She said before grabbing his arm to go inside.

A half hour later, and a with a full meal in her belly, Aubrey was ready to bring Sean up to date on the mysterious Maddie, along with her supposed relationship with William, and what William's daughter, Eileen, had told them.

Sean's eyebrows raised, he told her, "It really is a real life Nancy Drew mystery."

Aubrey gave him a snide look, "I'm serious, Sean, something bad happened to this girl, I just know it."

Nodding, Sean patted her hand, "I know, I'm sorry. I just find it difficult to think of when we really don't have all the pieces yet."

As if on cue, Aubrey's phone rang, she saw that it was Eileen Schultz and answered it right away, "Eileen, how are you?" She asked.

Eileen smiled, the girl was so nice. "I'm fine, dear, but you, oh you're in trouble!" She told Aubrey, adding in her customary dramatic flair.

"Why am I in trouble?" Aubrey asked her new friend.

While checking her hair in the entryway mirror, Eileen answered, "Oh, when I told Mother about the pictures, and your visit and questions, she was furious."

Oh Lord, Aubrey thought to herself. Now she would have a raving geriatric patient on her ass too! As if she'd said the words out loud, Aubrey gasped, and asked Eileen, "Oh, does that mean she won't see me?"

"On the contrary," Eileen informed her, "Her majesty, that's what I call Mother when she's in one of her holier than thou moods, requests your presence immediately."

Aubrey didn't know what to say, so she mumbled, "Uh, I don't know…." And trailed off.

As if understanding Aubrey's hesitation, Eileen let her know, "I'll accompany you, of course. I told her that you couldn't possibly see her until tomorrow, because you're famous, and that way, you can bring that sweet young man of yours too."

Biting her lip, Aubrey told Eileen, "I'll ask him." And then asked her, "What time tomorrow?"

After she hung up with Eileen, Aubrey sat there in shock for a full minute before Sean's waving hand permeated her foggy brain. "So," He asked her, "What was that about?"

Even as she was telling Sean about the meeting with the infamous Mrs. McIntyre, Aubrey knew she needed to see Cole and tell him. He'd been nothing but helpful to her and she was being a jerk to him.

She tried to call his cell phone on the way back from lunch, but she didn't get an answer.

When she arrived back at the house, all of his guys were gone, including him. She felt like maybe she'd really blown it with him, and he was trying to be nice to her by letting her down slowly.

Unlocking the back door, Aubrey went inside and threw her purse on the bar. She was about to turn around to go downstairs when she saw the note.

Picking up the paper, she saw the locket, and ran her fingers over the ornate edges. Using her nail, she opened it up and gasped at the images, tears streaking down her face. The two pictures were of Eileen and William, and Aubrey suspected that this was probably a gift from William to Maddie for that last Christmas.

She picked up the note again and read it,

*Aubrey,*

*Another piece of the puzzle. I'm here if you need me, I have to go into Racine to pick up some of your fixtures that came in, but I'll be back later.*

*Cole*

Smiling, Aubrey figured that maybe she hadn't quite messed things up as much as she thought.

# Chapter 24

When Cole got back to Aubrey's house, he was grumpy. Traffic was lousy, the fixtures he'd ordered didn't match what came in, so now he'd have to go back in a week to pick up the right ones. All of that, combined with this estrangement from Aubrey, was fraying his nerves.

He knocked before entering, wanting to give her time to tell him to go to hell. When he didn't hear anything, he opened the door. "Aubrey?" He called out.

"In here," Aubrey answered, from the living room.

He followed the sounds and found her, sitting on a blanket on the living room floor. She was wearing something silky, because it shimmered in the last bits of sunlight that snuck through the windows. "Uh," Cole stammered, "What are you doing?"

Standing up, Aubrey slowly crossed the space between them, and wrapped her arms around his neck. "Well, first," She nodded toward the blanket, "I'm going to feed you because they say the way to a man's heart is through his stomach," she leaned forward and kissed his chin, "And then I'm going to beg for forgiveness because I've been a mopey writer and you didn't deserve to be treated like that."

If Cole hadn't realized, the moment he saw her, how much he needed her, he would have realized it now. She made him feel alive, made him feel like he mattered, not because of what he did, but because of what they did together. "I didn't," He told her, trying to sound strict, "But I guess I have a lot to learn about moody writers."

Kissing him on the cheek, Aubrey whispered, "Tons," then kissed his nose, and then his lips.

Cole swept her up in his arms, and carried her over to the blanket.

They ate finger foods, fruit, cheese, crackers, and little eclairs she found at the grocery store. She had wine ready, but also had water in case he wasn't in a forgiving mood.

"This is nice," Cole told her, "Not exactly Cordon Bleu, but nice."

Aubrey tossed a grape at him, "This is all to butter you up, if I'm being completely honest."

Leaning forward, Cole asked, "For what?"

Picking up the locket, Aubrey rolled the grooved metal between her fingers, "I got a call from Eileen Schultz today, and her mother, Mrs. McIntyre wants to meet me tomorrow, and I'm hoping you'll come along."

"Of course," Cole told her, "I already explained," he leaned over and kissed her lips softly, "I'm in this all the way."

Trying to play devil's advocate, Aubrey offered, "I mean, she may not even tell us anything. She's not legally obligated to do so."

Cole shrugged, "Maybe not," he answered, "but at least you can say you tried, and Maddie can't fault you for that."

"You know," Aubrey told him, "Ever since I found this on the counter in the kitchen, I've felt better."

Intrigued, Cole asked her, "How's that?"

She stared at the locket, unable to put it down, "Like it's all calming down," she started to explain, "as if it were important to Maddie that we figured out who she was."

Smiling, Cole told her, "And that's a good thing."

"Yes it is," She responded.

They finished their meal and cleaned up the remnants, putting the blanket in the breakfast window seat, and the leftovers in the refrigerator. Aubrey was nervous, and stared at Cole, before asking, "Are you willing to stay here, with me?"

He saw her nervousness, and was having a healthy dose of his own, but he wouldn't leave her, not if she asked. "Of course," He answered, and they walked downstairs together.

The next morning, Aubrey and Cole drove out to Eileen Schultz's house. Cole offered to drive the women into Milwaukee, where Mrs. McIntyre was currently residing in an assisted living center.

As soon as Eileen saw them come up the drive, she came out onto the porch and waved. She was wearing purple today, about four different shades of it. Even though the outfit was colorful, it was still stylish. Aubrey couldn't help but smile when she got out of the car, and walked up to the porch to greet Eileen.

"Oh, my dears," Eileen crooned, giving Aubrey a kiss first, then Cole, as soon as he joined them. "Are you sure you want to do this?" She asked them. "Mother can be quite difficult."

Aubrey looked at Cole, "I think we can handle her," and they all started back down the porch stairs.

Cole made a show of putting Eileen in the sedan first, allowing her to sit up front with him. The woman practically swooned at his attentions, then he opened the door behind the driver's side, for Aubrey. She gave him a kiss and whispered, "Thank you," before getting in.

As Cole shut Aubrey's door, Eileen leaned back and said, "You've got a good one here," out of the side of her mouth, and Aubrey just nodded.

Eileen gave them directions into Milwaukee, and they chatted about a number of things. Finally Eileen asked Aubrey, "So where do you get your ideas for books, dear?"

Not aware that Eileen was familiar with her books, Aubrey asked, "Have you read them?"

Nodding, "Yes, a lady at the library, named Charlotte told me all about them, and they sounded fascinating, so I checked out one, and now I'm on the third one."

Impressed at her reading speed, Aubrey asked her, "Do you enjoy reading?"

Eileen sighed, "Dear, when you have an imagination like mine, and your children don't think you should be driving, you read!"

The tone in which Eileen spoke made both Aubrey and Cole laugh. The woman was an absolute delight!


It took about an hour to get to the assisted living center.

As Aubrey got out, allowing Cole to help Eileen out of her side of the car, she thought the place looked pretty swanky.

"It's nice isn't it?" Eileen asked her, as if she were reading her thoughts.

Nodding, Aubrey replied, "Yes, it is."

As if the sound of the words were distasteful, Eileen cringed as she said, "Mother always said she deserved the best, and that's what she's demanded all her life."

It was difficult for Aubrey to comprehend how Eileen used the word Mother, more as a label than as an endearing title. She would never use the word Mother like that when referring to her own mother. It was either, Mom, Mommy, or if she were in public and introducing her, she'd say, my mother, Christine, but she would never say it with such disdain.

"So," Cole turned to Eileen, patted her hand, and asked her, "What should we expect?"

They waited for the elevator in the lobby of the building. Everything was high end here, nothing was skimped on, but Aubrey felt like she wasn't allowed to touch anything either.

As the elevator doors closed, Eileen turned to Cole and answered his previous question with, "Hell, you can expect hell."

Her words sent a shiver down Aubrey's spine. She was on the other side of Eileen, and glanced over at Cole, who winked at her in an effort to reassure her it would be all be okay.

When the elevator doors opened, the three of them were greeted by a man dressed in a suit. He made a slight bow, and turned to Eileen, saying, "Good morning, Ms.

Eileen." And turned to look at Cole and Aubrey expectantly.

"Mr. Anthony," Eileen sounded formal, "these are mother's guests this morning, Ms. Aubrey Slojankonkowski and Mr. Cole Rafferty." She added, "Ms. Aubrey here is a famous mystery writer who writes as A.J. Sloan."

Again, Mr. Anthony made a slight bow, then said, "Please follow me, Mrs. McIntyre is in the parlor."

Aubrey felt like she'd just jumped in a time machine back to the 1800's with all the pomp and circumstance flying around this place. She scanned their surroundings and was notably impressed. There were original pieces of art from Rembrandt, and she thought even a piece of sculpture by Rodin, but she wasn't one hundred percent sure.

Finally, they were shown into a large room, full of gaudy furniture and littered with antiques. And there, in the corner, holding court, was Mrs. Marion McIntyre.

She didn't look one bit her eighty plus years, but Aubrey certainly wouldn't call her beautiful. Severe was the word that came to mind.

Mr. Anthony bowed to Mrs. McIntyre, then introduced them.

"Mother," Eileen said, and slowly made her way over. She air kissed her mother's cheek before retreating to the sofa that Aubrey and Cole now occupied.

Marion McIntyre scanned them up and down, "So," she said, her voice stern, "My daughter informs me that you wanted to speak with me regarding an old nanny we employed."

Aubrey looked over at Cole and then back to Mrs. McIntyre. The woman should work for the prison system, she could stop someone with only a look. "Yes, ma'am," She replied.

Eileen, trying to keep the conversation light, "They suspect that Father and Ms. Maddie were in a relationship."

The minute the words left her daughter's mouth, Marion's eyes grew dark. "A relationship?" She asked her daughter.

Watching the interaction between the two women, Aubrey was both upset and empathetic, at least on Eileen's behalf. To have to speak to your mother, as if you were begging for affection, it was humiliating, and it wasn't even her who it affected. Her stubborn streak coming out, Aubrey looked at Marion and said, "Mrs. McIntyre, we found letters and pictures and we believe that Maddie was the nanny who took care of Eileen when she was small. She disappeared just after that fire, at your husband's factory on Christmas Eve."

Marion McIntyre sat there, for at least a minute, glaring at the three of them. Then, she started to laugh.

Cole had never heard a laugh like this, it was cold, and menacing, and he felt protective of Aubrey and Eileen where this woman was concerned.

"That little slut!" Marion spit out, causing Aubrey, Eileen, and Cole to all stop and stare at her. "She thought she could come in and take my husband," her voice rose, "and my child!"

Eileen started to stand up, but Marion quickly motioned for her to sit down. Years of being beaten down, emotionally, had Eileen obeying.

Leaning forward, her eyes mere slits, Marion's face snarled, "Oh, I'll give William some credit, that little eel," she started, "thinking he could find some attorney in Chicago, that he could divorce me…."

Aubrey was silenced by the poison spilling out of this woman's mouth. It was unbelievable! She reached over and held Eileen's hand, feeling the woman shake with emotion.

"So, I fixed it," Marion told them, "I fixed it all."

Finally, years of trying to avoid the unpleasantness of her mother, made Eileen stand up, "What did you do?" She demanded, almost screaming at her mother. When Marion didn't answer, Eileen stomped over to her, and got in her face, "What did you do, Mother?" She yelled.

Marion, obviously not used to having anyone speak to her like that, replied, "I told him that his business was going down, I would see to it, so if he knew what was best for it, he'd burn it to the ground."

Aubrey looked over at Cole, still trying to process what was being said.

"What did you do?" Eileen screamed at Marion.

Clearly flustered, Marion tried to square her shoulders, "I sent a message to Maddie, telling her to meet him at the factory; I then told him to burn it down or I'd take it from him. And he did just that." She said, proud of herself for her scheming.

When the meaning of Marion's words permeated Eileen's brain, she staggered backward. Cole shot up from where he was sitting, and guided her to the closest chair. Tears were streaming down her face, "You told him to burn down the factory, when you knew she was in there?" Eileen asked in a shaky voice.

Looking away, Marion ignored her daughter.

"Mother, answer the question!" Eileen demanded.

Brushing her hand in front of her face, as if she were slapping at a bug, Marion responded, "Yes," Her voice was extremely calm, almost icy, "Yes, I did  And I'd do it again,

I tell you" She responded. "Oh, he was devastated when his poor little dear wasn't in the house the next morning. It didn't take him long to figure out what happened." She sat there, her voice devoid of emotion, and told them, "He told me that I would rot in hell and he would never stay married to me." She laughed then, the sadistic sound echoed around the room. "I told him, the only thing that would split us up was the grave, so, two months later, he took a pistol from my father's gun case when we were visiting Chicago, and he shot himself in the head."

Eileen, clearly devastated by this revelation, started crying uncontrollably. "You told me," She pointed at her mother, "that he had a heart attack."

Unaffected by her daughter's display of emotion, Marion replied, "It was easy enough to cover up, I paid the doctor and the coroner."

Aubrey felt sick. This woman actually thought that all the horrible actions she took were justified. "What about Maddie?" She demanded of Marion.

"What about her?" Marion spat back, "She died in that fire, and like the whore she was, is now burning in hell for her sins. She's the one who brought this all on, getting pregnant by a married man!"

The last statement had Aubrey, Cole, and Eileen actually shocked once again.

Eileen stood, patting Cole's hand as he stood by her, "I will never see you again after today, you are a wretched person and you are the one who has to fear burning in hell."

Pointing a skinny finger at her daughter, Marion countered, "Oh, you'll change your tune. I won't be here much longer and you'll want the money."

"Actually, Mother," Eileen spat out the words, "I don't need your money, Grandfather, Father, and Jim left me enough that my children, hell my grandchildren, will be taken care of, so you can shove your money!" She grabbed her bag and started to leave the room.

Marion called after her, "You'll be back; you always are!"

At the doorway of the room, Eileen turned around to say, "I came back because you're my mother and I actually felt sorry for you." She was crying now, "I see that you never had a heart so it was impossible for you to love and to have someone love you back. As far as Father, I think he did what he had to do to get away from you!"

Finally realizing that what her daughter said was no idle threat, Marion started to show a crack in her composure. She slumped forward, but wouldn't stop staring her daughter down. She didn't say anything else before the three of them left.

The elevator ride down, was quiet.  No one knew what to say.  None of them expected to be told what they were told, and Aubrey wanted to cry for poor Maddie and William.  Putting her hand in her pocket, Aubrey's fingers brushed the metal of the locket.  She pulled it out, and handed it to Eileen.  "Here," She said, "this was found behind a brick in the fireplace, and I think it was something your father was going to give to Maddie for Christmas."

Eileen accepted the piece of jewelry, and her eyes filled with tears.  "No," She said to Aubrey, "Father and I gave this to Maddie for her birthday just a few weeks before Christmas."

Aubrey looked over at Cole, tears of her own spilling down her cheeks.

# Chapter 25

Four weeks later……

Late May was warm, almost hot, and Aubrey was nervous as she drove out Hwy 36 North. She made the turn to go into the nearby town of Waterford. It, like Burlington, hadn't changed in some ways, but grew up in others. She made the turn left and passed the high school. There was a gas station that she hadn't noticed before, and a large subdivision where there was once a farmer's field. She passed a restaurant that was a converted barn, and smiled.

A couple of miles up ahead, she turned into a small cemetery.

There were a few cars there, including Cole's and she looked at the time, concerned that she was late. She wasn't, so that was a relief.

Stepping out of the vehicle, she gave a smile to Cole and met him a few yards away. "Good morning," She said to him, sadness lacing her words.

"Good morning to you," He returned, and gave her a kiss.

They walked over to where a new stone was laid, and waited for the Pastor to speak.

"Good morning to everyone here," He started. "We're here today to lay to rest, Madalyn Wilkins, or Maddie as

she was known." He read a passage from his Bible, and
then asked, "Is there anyone who would like to say a few
words?"

Eileen Schultz stepped forward, and held a piece of
paper in her hands, she winked at Aubrey, and then said,
"This letter was from Maddie's love, William, and it
reads.....

*My Dearest:*

*You are the brightest part of my day, you are the reason I know
I've found love, and you are the glue that holds my daughter and
I together in this otherwise, spinning world of insanity. Know
that my thoughts are with you every second of every day. I will
always be with you, no matter what.*

*All My Love*

As Eileen stepped away, tears in her eyes, Aubrey
reached out and squeezed her shoulder as a sign of
support. The Pastor said a few more words, and then the
small gathering dispersed.


Aubrey was standing with Cole and Eileen when a
woman came over to them, "Hello," she said to them, "I'm
Madelyn Wilkins."

The three of them were silent. Not only did this
woman look almost identical to the woman in the pictures,

but she had the same name. For a moment, Aubrey thought they were talking to a ghost.

Madelyn told them, "My father, James, was Maddie's younger brother, and named me after her."

Eileen stepped forward, and hugged the woman, "I want you to know," she said to Madelyn, "that your aunt was loved, truly loved."

Nodding, Madelyn told her, "Yes, she was."

The two women walked over to where the headstone was placed and spoke.

Aubrey turned to Cole, "I think she's gone now," she said, "from the house."

Cole looked at her, "I think so too," he added. "Are you ready for tonight?" He asked as he walked her over to her car.

"I think so," She answered as she dabbed her eyes. "I've got the caterers set, Mom is doing the whole thing basically, so I just have to go to the airport and pick up my friends."

Nodding, Cole asked her, "Do you want me to come with?"

Aubrey shook her head, and said, "No thanks, I've got it," before kissing him on the cheek and getting into the car.

Cole stood there in the cemetery and watched her drive away.

A lot had happened since that day they found out the real story about Maddie and William, and none of them had been the same since.

Aubrey and Eileen discussed whether or not they should actually go to the District Attorney with Marion's confession, but without a body and proof, it would be tough. Marion's life would be over within a few short years anyway, so they felt it was better to use their efforts for other purposes.

They hired a private investigator to track down Maddie's family, and tell them what had happened. Eileen insisted on paying for the funeral, and made sure it was here, at this cemetery, because it's where William was buried. Now their headstones would be right next to one another.

Cole had finished the house, ahead of schedule, and helped Aubrey plan for the housewarming party she had set up for tonight.

Everything was good, except that, since finding out Maddie's fate, Aubrey was distant. She tried to blame it on her writing, since she was now on the second book of the new series, but he knew that wasn't all. They hadn't made love since that first night, at his house, and he wondered if she just didn't want him anymore.

Seeing Eileen coming his way, he pasted on his smile, and escorted her to the car so he could take her home.

"You know," Eileen chatted as they drove along the country road, "Aubrey is madly in love with you."

Cole wanted to laugh, the way she said it was like she said those things every day. "I'm not sure about that."

Sighing Eileen, said, "Now, you listen here young man. That girl is scared. She told me what that psychic friend of hers said, parallel loves, and all that stuff. She's afraid Cole, afraid that your love will end, just like Maddie and my father's."

"That's absurd," Cole replied in a terse tone, then corrected himself, remembering the company he was in, "I apologize, and I guess I just don't see it that way."

Eileen shook her head, "Men!" She exclaimed, "Always wanting things to be so cut and dried, when women are far more complicated."

He pulled into her driveway, and got out to get her door. Eileen patted his cheek with her palm and smiled.

"The thing about love," Eileen explained as he escorted her up to the porch, "Is that it's the messiest, craziest, most encompassing thing, and it makes absolutely no sense whatsoever."

Cole was about to walk away when he turned back to Eileen, and said "There's still something I don't understand."

Eileen smiled, and asked him, "What's that dear?"

Sighing, Cole said, "That rocking chair, why was it in the fruit cellar?"

Wearing a knowing look, Eileen answered, "When I misbehaved, or Mother deemed me as bad, she would put me in the fruit cellar." She let a tear slip down her cheek, and added, "All I remember is being rocked in that rocking chair and not being so scared."

As he walked back to his car, Cole knew that they would never move that rocking chair.


Aubrey was standing in the entryway of her house, nerves filling up her gut. "Oh, why did I agree to this?" She asked no one.

Christine happened to be walking out of the dining room, and answered, "Because it will be fun."

Not sure, Aubrey tried to put on a smile. "I hope so, I should've talked to Cole, to make sure he was coming."

"Cole's not coming?" Greg asked as he came into the end of the conversation.

Shrugging, Aubrey replied, "I don't know. He helped me plan it, but he's been distant."

Giving her husband a knowing look, that told him to scram, Christine turned and led her daughter over to the staircase, and they sat down on the third stair. "Has it been Cole who's been distant? Or you?" She asked her daughter.

Blowing out a breath, Aubrey answered, "It's been me. I love him, Mom, and I know exactly how Maddie felt, I'm just afraid of it all ending."

Cole was in the dining room, when he heard the conversation between Aubrey and her mother. Stepping into the entryway, "Did I make you feel like it was going to end?" He asked Aubrey.

Shocked, Aubrey jumped up from her seat on the stair, and absently brushed her hands down her dress. "Uh, no, I just..."

He smiled, and walked up to her, "It won't you know, not if we don't let it." Turning, Cole looked at Aubrey's parents, who now stood behind them. "I'd like to ask you both for your permission to marry your daughter."

Greg rolled his eyes, and responded, "Please do, she's driving us nuts," to which he received a jab in the side by his wife for saying it.

As Aubrey stood there, Cole reached in his pocket, and pulled out a ring. It was beautiful, and looked antique.

"Eileen gave me this, she found it among her father's things and figured that he'd probably been planning on giving it to Maddie when he married her."

Aubrey's fingers shook as she gave him her hand and slid the ring on her finger. It fit perfectly.

Looking into her blue eyes, Cole said, "Now, we will live in this beautiful house that just cost you a small fortune to bring back to life, and you and I will raise our own kids and throw parties," he leaned down and kissed her, "and we'll be happy, I promise you, Aubrey, because I love you."

She tried to keep the tears from falling, since she had makeup on.

Just then the doorbell rang. Christine answered it and it was Sean, Eileen, and Aubrey's friends from California.

Eileen spoke first, when she saw the situation, "Oh, oh, he gave you the ring, does this mean that you said yes?" She asked eagerly.

"She hasn't said anything yet," Cole told them, and everyone was quiet.

Aubrey looked around her, the faces of the people she loved, and her beautiful house were exactly what she needed. "Yes," She whispered. "I'll marry you Cole."

Cheers erupted, and everyone migrated to the dining room, where waiters were starting to pour champagne.

Downstairs, in the fruit cellar, the rocking chair started to rock, and a woman's laughter filled the silence.

Dear Readers:

This book is so dear to me, and is truly a family affair. My leading lady is named after my daughter-in-law and my dad, Mike, helped me come up with the idea years ago, when we lived in the house on Duane Street that's in the story. There are so many memories intertwined in the story that it's been an emotional journey for me to write it. The story is fiction though and not based on any real people.

Thank you to the City of Burlington, for being a hometown I'm proud of. Thank you to my high school friends who were "Okay" with me putting them in the book. A very special Thank You to the businesses that agreed to let me use them in the book as well, I think it brings a sense of home to the city, which happens to be an important character in this story.

"We spend our childhood trying to get away from our hometown, and spend our adulthood trying to recapture the magic of it." ~ Danette Fogarty

www.ingramcontent.com/pod-product-compliance
Lightning Source LLC
Chambersburg PA
CBHW061426040426
42450CB00007B/922